Internet
Safety Guide

Empowering children to protect themselves online through education

Zeeko Internet Safety Guide

Copyright © 2016 Caraglass Ltd. All rights reserved

Published by Zeeko, Dublin, Ireland

Limit of Liability/ Disclaimer of Warranty: While the publisher and author have used their best efforts in preparing this book, they make no representations or warranties with respect to the accuracy or completeness of the contents of this book and specifically disclaim any implied warranties of merchantability or fitness for a particular purpose. No warranty may be created or extended by sales representatives or written sales materials. The advice and strategies contained herein may not be suitable for your situation. You should consult with a professional where appropriate. Neither the publisher nor author shall be liable for any loss of profit or any other commercial damages, including but not limited to special, incidental, consequential, or other damages For more copies of this book, please email: joe@zeeko.ie, Tel: +353-(01)-5312612

For more information about Zeeko resources, visit our web site at www.zeeko.ie

ISBN 978-0-9934659-0-1

ZEEKO INTERNET SAFETY GUIDE

Empowering parents through education to protect their kids online

Claire O'Broin

Emma Kenny

Maria O'Loughlin

Joe Kenny

Aisling O'Hagan

ZEEKO *Internet Safety Guide*

❝ It was excellent - our pupils learned some very useful tips on safety, how to keep safe and where their responsibilities lay. Highly recommended ❞

Mary O'Leary, Principal, St. Helen's SNS, Portmarnock

❝ All parents should do this course so as they stay one step ahead of their kids ❞

Anne - Margaret attended a Parent Crash Course in July

❝ Claire and Aisling have educated me thoroughly this evening on the subject of Internet Safety. Having 2 young teenagers learning and being informed is a big help. Ignorance is not bliss when it comes to the internet. The girls did an excellent job ❞

Louise attended a Parent Crash Course in July

❝ The evidence based material and research ensured a thoroughly interesting dialogue between facilitator and audience. It takes the "mystery" out of social media. The rules were excellent and easily remembered ❞

James Tobin, Principal, Holy Trinity NS, Leopardstown

❝ I found the course very informative. I definitely want to be a proactive parent - thankfully I have time on my side for a change ❞

Elaine attended a Parent Crash Course in July

❝ A must-attend for any parent ❞

Marc attended a Parent Crash Course in July

❝ Maria gave us a very thought - provoking presentation and our boys really responded to the Stop Block Tell and 5:1 rules ❞

Maureen Fitzpatrick, Principal, St. Joseph's CBS, Fairview

❝Superbly done - really engaged the children, brilliantly presented & a great presentation for parents. The whole concept is exceptional. Should be mandatory in every school. Research bang up to date ❞

Jerry Grogan, Principal, Holy Trinity NS, Donaghmede

FACES OF ZEEKO

Joe and Linda Kenny
Founders of Zeeko

My wife, Linda and I believe the internet is a fantastic resource for our son. Equally we believe that children should be safe online. We do not agree with all the hurt and extreme consequences created in young peoples' lives due to the internet. In 2013 we decided to work to correct this.

Initially we thought the solution was a technical solution. But people asked us how a technical solution could protect their children when their children could use a device other than their own to access the internet, for example using a computer in a friend's house on a play date. Hence, we quickly released the primary solution had to be through education.

We provide resources to children, parents and teachers on internet safety. We have come to realise that teachers and parents have a sense of helplessness when it comes to protecting their children online. Frequently we hear from parents that they feel their children are far more proficient at using the internet than they are as parents. Our children maybe more technically efficient but they do not have the maturity to make informed decisions on how to behave online.

We have worked on this project for over 2 years. We have invested a substantial amount of our own money in the project. Our primary objective is to raise awareness about online safety and to help parents and teachers empower their children to protect themselves online. We are developing an app to introduce children to safe online communication. We will continue to work hard to bring about change through education. We hope you find this book informative and helpful.

Maria O'Loughlin
Seminar Presenter
- *Parent of 2 children*
- *Degree in Psychology and MSc in Computers & Information Systems*
- *Over 20 years customer service and sales experience*

Claire O'Broin
Digital Specialist
- *Diploma in Digital Marketing*
- *Member of the European Institute of Communications (MEIC)*
- *Background in social media management*
- *Currently studying for a Masters in Marketing in the UCD Michael Smurfit School of Business*

FACES OF ZEEKO

Emma Kenny
Lead Animator
- Studied Game Development in Pulse College
- Previously lead animator for an Irish online Educational Game and App

Aisling O Hagan
Social Media Specialist
- Background in Marketing and Sales
- Holds a Masters in Marketing from UCD Michael Smurfit School of Business
- Fundraiser for children's charity in spare time

Acknowledgements

I am indebted to Claire, Emma, Aisling and Maria for your joint efforts in writing this book. Thanks to Michelle, Zoe, Louise, Grainne, Louise and Davina for your help in getting this book published. I am thankful to the schools that facilitate our research and help us propagate our educational message.

I am grateful to Aileen and Marie Therese for their help in raising awareness about the book. A special thanks to Grainne for your oversight and willingness always to help. Thanks to Raomal for perpetually questioning our direction. I would like to thank Fredericka for consistently finding answers and helping me drive on.

Thanks to Joe and Rita for cultivating their egalitarian ethos and belief that everything is possible. Linda and Ciarán, thanks for your unconditional support of my entrepreneurial ventures. Without every one of you this would not have been possible.

Table of Contents

1	Your Child's Digital Footprint	23
2	Safely Social	31
3	How to Talk to your Child in their Language	45
4	The Virtual School Yard Bully	57
5	Stranger Danger	89
6	Hopscotch to Headsets	99
7	Excessive Internet Use	111
8	Safety Settings	121
9	Devices	135
10	Inappropriate Content	189
11	The Resource Hub	201
12	Endnotes	209
13	Appendix	213
14	Index	219

Foreword

By Dr Grainne Kirwan Cyber Psychology Specialist, IADT, Dublin.

Online interactions today may sometimes seem to be a minefield, especially for young people and their parents who are concerned about Internet safety. The temptation might be to prevent children from accessing online technologies entirely, in what may be a well-intentioned but misguided attempt to protect them from the various dangers online. Nevertheless, without the opportunity to explore the benefits of Internet technologies, young people today may find themselves seriously disadvantaged both socially and educationally, and a lack of appropriate skills may result in reduced career options as they grow older. Online activities such as social media and gaming have been found to have many benefits for young people, including enhancement of interpersonal relationships and social interaction, expression of identity, enhanced self-esteem, self-affirmation, leadership skills, cognitive benefits, and many more. The solution is not to prevent young people from accessing the Internet, but rather to help them to learn how to use the technologies in the best possible way, so that they can grow and develop the skills required for living in a world where the Internet is no longer a new and unusual space, but rather an integrated element of many aspects of daily life. Preventing young people from accessing online resources because of the potential dangers involved is equivalent to banning them from ever travelling in a motor vehicle or crossing the road because of the potential dangers inherent in those activities. A complete ban on internet activity might reduce the possibility of negative consequences from online sources, but it will definitely impair their ability to develop and reach their potential in educational, occupational and social settings. Instead of attempting to ban young people from the internet, a far more preferable approach is to recognise the similarity between road safety and internet safety - guide children on how to behave in online environments to reduce risk, and provide support for their problems and questions, in the same way that we teach them how to cross the road safely and, eventually, how to drive.

The Zeeko Internet Safety Guide provides tangible and specific advice on how parents, teachers, and others can protect children online, without unnecessarily impairing children's development. Indeed, the authors recognise the dangers in imposing bans on using technologies, as children can easily access the Internet through other means, and if anything does go wrong, they may then be considerably less likely to seek the help and support that they need as they fear the punishment that may occur if they tell their parents that they have been online without permission. A child who has been banned from Internet use is doubly at risk - they lack the knowledge and skills to use the resources in the safest and best way, and they are more limited in who they can seek help from. The Zeeko Guide advocates a more appropriate response - aiding parents to encourage appropriate online use and clear communication, as well as providing guidance and suggestions that are easy for young people to understand and follow. The step-by-step instructions with screenshots included in the Guide will help parents and teachers to feel more confident as they configure devices to improve safety and privacy, while also removing some of the potential confusion which may arise as adults try to navigate the online resources and media that are used extensively by young people. This has the added benefit of increasing the likelihood that young people will approach their parents, teachers, or other appropriate adults for advice if anything does go amiss online - the guide advocates an open and honest channel of communication, and provides specific suggestions on how to achieve this. I believe that any parent who is concerned about their child's online safety should read this guide, and that it will be an invaluable source of advice and suggestions which can be consulted over and over again.

Introduction

As parents in the Digital Age, we are all concerned about our children's safety when using the Internet. With so many Wi-Fi enabled devices at our children's fingertips, from iPads and smartphones, to games consoles and iPods, we as parents need to be fully equipped to keep our children out of harm's way when using the Internet. Throughout our research and in the course of our work, education has constantly proven to be the most valuable asset to parents and children alike in online safety.

Because of this, we at Zeeko have put together this Internet Safety Guide to help all parents, regardless of digital proficiency, to get to grips with the online world facing our children. As parents ourselves, we know that time is scarce, so this Guide is intended to be a quick, easy and a user-friendly read. From cyberbullying to all things social media, we have it covered!

Chapter 1 looks at Digital Footprints – what they are, and how you can keep your child's digital footprint positive and harmless. Many parents are extremely concerned about the potentially negative repercussions of their child being active on social media, and the range and functionality of various platforms can be mindboggling, so Chapter 2 helps you get to grips with social media and how to manage it effectively in your home.

Speaking the 'cyber language' that is so familiar to many of our kids is one of the top challenges for many parents – knowing your 'story' (Snapchat) from your 'favourite' (Instagram) can be a minefield, but Chapter 3 condenses all of this down and helps you grasp your child's digital lingo.

Cyberbullying is by far one of the biggest concerns for parents and schools alike, and whether your child is the victim or the bully, we address this issue in Chapter 4 – from the different types of cyberbully, to equipping your child with our simple rule to combat cyberbullying (Stop, Block, Tell!).

Digital Stranger Danger is a topic often sensationalised in the media, and the prospect of your child interacting with a potentially sinister stranger online can be terrifying. However, in compiling our All Ireland Digital Trend Report with children aged 7-13, we have learned that quite a large proportion are interacting with strangers online (playing against them, friending or following them on social media or even chatting to them on games or sites with a chat function). Chapter 5 offers you some simple steps to help you equip your child with the knowledge and tools to keep safe from this digital threat.

Chapter 6 explores the popularity of online gaming amongst children (big and small!), the potential risks associated with online gaming and how to avoid these. We also discuss two of the most popular games among this age group (7-13 years old), their suitability and content, and suggest a fantastic resource to check the appropriateness of a game before you purchase or allow your child to play, as well as offering some child-friendly alternatives.

Excessive internet use is considered a relatively new issue. It is obviously one that parents need to be fully aware of. We look at this issue in depth in

Chapter 7, from the signs that your child may be developing excessive use to their time online, to our easy-to-remember prevention tool; the 5:1 Rule.

While they are not a substitute for education about online safety, safety settings are very useful in helping to protect our kids. In Chapter 8 we review the tools available to you from Internet providers, mobile phone operators, various websites and search engines, and some of the apps and software programmes specifically designed to safeguard against cyber threats. Then in Chapter 9, we turn our attentions to devices themselves; iOS devices (iPhone, iPad, iPod), Android devices (phones and tablets), Windows and Mac computers.

Finally, in Chapter 10, we tackle the issue of inappropriate content. Although what that term covers can vary from parent to parent (depending on the age and maturity of their children), the underlying principles remain the same when it comes to dealing with this cyber threat in your home and we offer some simple, yet effective, steps that any parent can implement.

All in all, this Guide aims to provide simple advice and easy-to-implement steps, to equip parents with the knowledge they need to empower their children to stay safe online.

1

Your Child's Digital Footprint

An Introduction to Online Safety

As parents today, it is likely that you made your first mark on the Internet roughly 15 years ago.

When your name is typed into an online search bar, there is a good chance that a social media profile will pop up; your latest tweets, perhaps your Facebook profile picture and maybe your LinkedIn account. Imagine if your digital footprint had started as a child, and imagine how different this search would look today. Your children's digital footprint can start before they begin to walk and follow them around for life. As a parent, you are responsible for what has become known as your child's 'digital footprint', or 'digital shadow'.

Today's technology means children can have a social media presence before they are old enough in the eyes of the law to have a say on whether or not they want one.

> *"As a parent, you are responsible for what has become known as your child's digital shadow"*

For many parents, knowing how to protect their child's digital footprint is a minefield. We have conducted considerable research with parents and teachers to listen to your concerns. We have visited schools across Ireland, meeting pupils to find out more about current online trends. We have drawn upon our own backgrounds in social media, digital technology and psychology, and combined all of this to bring you the 'Zeeko Internet Safety Guide'. Throughout this book, we will be giving you full insights into your child's online world and advice on how to protect them in cyberspace.

One important trend we at Zeeko have observed is that when children go online they are increasingly ***going mobile***. Tablets are the most commonly used devices amongst primary school children, with 39% of 1st class primary school children saying they use a tablet[1]. The danger with this trend is that children can be accessed by strangers or bullies anytime, anywhere. This is coupled with the ever-increasing popularity of Wi-Fi enabled devices, e.g. iPods, iPads and Xbox consoles. Wi-Fi enabled devices allow children to access online games with chat functions, social networking sites and chat apps.

---

[1] Source: Zeeko All Ireland Digital Trend Report

Children no longer need a phone to engage with friends as they can simply use a chat app or visit their social media profile on a Wi-Fi enabled device, such as an iPod.

The age children engage with the internet today is getting much younger. Children up to 3rd class enjoy a variety of online activities, including watching videos, playing games, searching for information, doing their homework and socialising within virtual worlds. Entertainment remains the most popular online activity amongst all age categories, although the range of activities increases with age. As children reach 4th, 5th and 6th classes, they begin to interact with social media sites, chat apps and online games. Examples of these include Instagram, Snapchat and FIFA. With 6th class pupils in primary schools in Ireland using these apps to the following extent: 43% using Instagram; 37% using Snapchat, and 8% using FIFA.[2]

Although the majority of activity is relatively innocent and innocuous, there are some associated threats attached to even the most seemingly innocent sites, which when ignored, can put your child in danger. The key threats to children when using age appropriate virtual worlds are the exposure and contact from strangers through fake profiles. Exposure to inappropriate

"Perhaps the most overlooked benefit of a child using the Internet is that it helps them to develop their digital literacy"

---

[2] Source: Zeeko All Ireland Digital Trend Report

content is a primary concern for many parents. When surfing the net for homework or games or looking for something on YouTube, children can be exposed to inappropriate content, which comes in many forms (from inappropriate advertising to drugs and violence). As kids progress to use social media, chat apps and online gaming, the risk of contact from strangers increases. In addition, the threat of cyberbullying is constantly increasing as more of their peers move online.

Your child will have a number of positive reasons for using the Internet: education, entertainment and socialising with friends. Cyberspace offers a vast range of positive elements for our children. It lets them communicate with friends and family. It can even support children in accomplishing new goals such as coding, designing a poster or creating a video to share with friends and family. Perhaps the most overlooked benefit of a child using the Internet is that it helps them to develop their digital literacy, which has become a vital life skill in itself. With so many day-to-day tasks moving online (banking, shopping, travel, research etc.), the Internet has integrated itself into our personal, academic and professional lives. Despite the threats, there is no doubt that the Internet has become an essential part of a child's upbringing, and their subsequent development, and so, mitigating the risks in order to protect our children is our ultimate goal.

At Zeeko we advise parents to practice active mediation when it comes to digital parenting. Give your child the tools and education that they need to protect themselves against threats on the internet. Allow them to reap the benefits of the internet for education, entertainment and safe communication. Empower them to be a responsible Internet user, to be comfortable talking about their online endeavours and perhaps most importantly, to speak up if they are confronted with any issues or challenges without fear of severe punishment. Our 'Internet Safety Guide' will give you step-by step-advice across a range of topics, on how to protect your child online and have peace of mind that they are safe.

The Zeeko Mantra

"Treat the Internet like a noticeboard"

Generally speaking, the content you post on the Internet cannot be easily removed or deleted. This is true for social networks, chat apps and photo sharing sites. Before you or your child post content online, ask yourself, "Would I post this on a public noticeboard?"

KEY TAKEAWAYS

- ☑ As a parent, you are responsible for your child's 'digital shadow'
- ☑ The internet can help kids develop their digital literacy, which has become a vital life skill
- ☑ Treat the internet like a noticeboard

2

Safely Social

Explain to your child that they should act on social media as they do in real life; with respect and dignity

It can be difficult to keep up to date with the social networks that are on your child's radar, as there are new platforms constantly emerging. Whether your child is digitally active or not, the chances are that they know all about Snapchat, Instagram and Viber.

For parents, social media can seem mindboggling with all of the various platforms and how they function, and how quickly the app of the moment can change. However, this chapter will get you up to speed on all things social media, from your child's introduction to it and their presence on social platforms, to helping you get to grips with the latest platforms.

General Tips:

- Most social network sites comply with the Children's Online Privacy Protection Act (COPPA), and rather than collecting verifiable consent from parents for kids under 13, they simply restrict usage to those over 13 to avoid the issue. In many of our talks, the majority of kids have admitted to lying about their age to get around this when joining a platform

- Respect on social media is a fundamental matter. There is often a disconnection for kids between real life and their digital world, which can cause them to do things online that they would never do in real life. Explain to your child that they should act on social media as they do in real life; with respect and dignity

- It's vital to speak to your child before they join any social media sites, and talk about the potential risks. Educate them about responsible usage, what to do if they encounter any issues and discuss what platform might suit them best. We would always recommend that they start their social media journey with a child-friendly app, which has appropriate safety settings and features

- Familiarise yourself with the platform that your child is joining, and know its features and capabilities. Then sit down with your child to set up their profile, ensure that it is set to private so they are not visible to strangers, and that their profile does not contain any overly personal information or images which could leave them vulnerable

- Sit down regularly with your child for them to show you around their profiles. This empowers them to work with you towards a safer social media experience as opposed to against you. Try not to have a set time and day that you do it, as you run the risk of your child removing content, settings or friends that they don't want you to see, if they know that you always check at a specific time

- Keep track of your child's password. You should be able to check it whenever you feel the need to, and a condition of them being on any social networks should be that they inform you of any password changes

- Have a cut-off time for social media and general phone use in the evening. The Yale Medical Group recommends that all devices are switched off at least an hour before bedtime, to avoid the blue light technology interfering with your child's sleep patterns and even their alertness the following day.

Generating Content

- A growing trend among children is content generation. Photo and video content is particularly popular amongst children, and has never been easier to generate, with cameras on their phones and tablets. Many will share their content on Facebook, Instagram, Snapchat and YouTube. The danger here is that children can expose personal information such as their school, their address, and their routines to a public audience, leaving them highly vulnerable. The advice here is to encourage children to take videos if this is a hobby of theirs, but ask that they verify them with you before they upload, and only to share them with friends and family.

Speak their language

- Show kids you're interested in speaking their language and understanding their digital world. When kids allow you into their digital world, you can understand their feelings towards it. Are they happy when they talk about their activity on social media, do they show any anxiety, are they very secretive? It is important to have these regular conversations to ensure you are monitoring your child's relationship with the Internet. Some examples are below:

- o "Did you favourite anything today? Follow anyone new today?"
- o "Any good 'snaps' today? Who are your 'top friends' on Snapchat?"
- o "Any news from your groups on WhatsApp today? Who is in the group chat?

Social Networking – What You Need to Know

 Instagram

- Instagram is the most popular social networking app among children we have spoken with. With the following percentages of children using Instagram: 0% of 1st class; 3% of 2nd class; 9th of 3rd class; 16% of 4th class; 24% of 5th Class, and 43% of 6th Class[3]
- It is a media editing and sharing app, which facilitates interaction through taking, editing, sharing, and commenting on photos and videos
- While a lot of the usage is very innocent, there are of course risks associated with Instagram. Inappropriate content is a primary threat on the platform, as many kids follow celebrities (such as Rihanna, Miley Cyrus, Kylie Jenner, Mario Balotelli and Kim Kardashian) that post inappropriate and explicit content
- Some are also using the platform to engage in cyberbullying, through nasty or aggressive comments underneath photos
- For many kids, amassing a large number of followers is part and parcel of Instagram, so it is vital to discuss with your child the associated dangers of having strangers following your child
- Instagram's default profile setting is public, but it is relatively easy to make private (see Chapter 8 on Safety Settings). Posts can also be

---

[3] Source: Zeeko All Ireland Digital Trend Report

made private, and viewable only to the followers you have approved to view them
- It is important to be aware that anyone who followed you before you set the profile to private will still be able to see all content posted (even if you don't follow them), unless you specifically block them.

 Snapchat

- Very popular among children in the 4th class and above age category
- Children take a picture or video, and send it to their Snapchat friends
- The photo or video disappears after a chosen time of between 1 and 10 seconds
- While many kids and teens use it for the spontaneity factor, to share with a friend fun images that will disappear, this app now poses a few risks

- There are a few workarounds which prevent the photo or video disappearing after the selected time – a simple screenshot of the picture can be saved (the sender is notified that it has been taken) or unaffiliated apps such as SnapSave and SnapCrack save each and every Snapchat received by the recipient in question to their camera roll, without the sender receiving a notification. There is also an option to replay 'snaps'
- It can also be a popular means for cyberbullying, as the evidence disappears (or is supposed to disappear) as soon as it has displayed for a maximum of 10 seconds

Facebook

- 5% of primary school children use Facebook[4]
- Facebook has a 'real names' policy, meaning that most kids display their full names on their profile. Profile photos don't have to show a child's face, but 83% of kids report that their profile photo does show their face
- The platform has a huge range of functionality, from facilitating conversation and sharing photos and videos, to reviewing restaurants and supporting charitable causes
- Facebook has certain safety settings for users aged between 13 and 18, such as restricting advertising for items such as alcohol, dietary

---

[4] Source: Zeeko All Ireland Digital Trend Report

supplements, online gambling sites and other inappropriate content. However, as a lot of younger kids lie about their age to join Facebook (as they are under the required age of 13), they often set it to being quite a bit older, and so, may be exposed to this content, and not protected by the limited safety settings put in place by Facebook

- Again, as with most platforms, it can be used to cyberbully and engage in nasty or inappropriate behaviour. Peer harassment is the most common threat associated with Facebook

With all of this said, are there any positives to allowing your child on social media? Well, we have found a number of positives that can come from children using social media on a supervised basis, as reported by parents, psychologists and kids themselves. At an age where they are beginning to shape their own identity and discovering who they are as a person, many kids like being able to express themselves on their social profile. From their musical tastes to pictures and videos that relate to their identity, it often offers a less daunting means of self-expression than doing so face to face with people. However, it is vital that children understand that divulging too much personal information can be dangerous, and that impulsive posting about other people and certain matters can be inappropriate, harmful to friendships and have far-reaching consequences in all aspects of their life.

In addition, for children who find it difficult to interact with their peers, or who feel isolated, it can be a way of connecting. It can help shy and withdrawn children to communicate and feel part of the group, and they can take the communication and interaction skills that they develop on social media offline to the real world to benefit them there.

The primary reason we hear from kids as to why they think social media is positive boils down to communication. Many of the children we speak to use it to stay in touch with family or friends that live far away, as many of us do, as well as friends and family closer afield.

It can often offer an excellent introduction to the digital world when introduced in a controlled and safe environment, where you monitor their activity and work with your child to help them become a responsible Internet user. It can essentially serve as a tool to aid their digital, and overall, development.

At what age should I allow my child on social media?

This is by far the question we hear the most in relation to this topic, as parents are torn between keeping their child offline for as long as possible and not wanting their child to feel excluded or the odd one out. The simple answer is that there is no right answer – there is no definitive age at which your child is ready for social media.

We believe it depends on the child's maturity and personal development as to when they are ready to venture into the world of social media, and you as a parent are the best judge of this. When they begin asking about setting up a social profile, have the conversation about why they want to become active on social media, and how they think it is appropriate to use it. Ask them how they would react in certain situations to ensure they will practice the **Stop, Block, Tell** rule in the event of a negative situation arising.

If you feel they are showing a sufficient level of responsibility and maturity, you should agree on some ground rules for social media usage, such as the platform they can use, the times they can access it, random spot checks and keeping you informed of their login credentials. Write these down and then agree on some sanctions or consequences in the event of any of the agreed rules being broken – we recommend something along the lines of access times being reduced, or access privileges being withdrawn temporarily after a discussion surrounding the wrongdoing. This allows your child to feel part of the decision-making process and gives them the responsibility and accountability for their own privileges or lack thereof.

Ultimately, it is your decision as a parent as to when is the right time for your child to go onto social media, but the above measures should give you a good indication of whether they are ready.

KEY TAKEAWAYS

- ☑ Before your child joins any social media platform, have the conversation about why they want to use social media, how they deem it appropriate to use it and establish some agreed ground rules
- ☑ Familiarise yourself with the platform they will be using so you can help them and monitor their activity
- ☑ There is no right age for your child to join social networking platforms – it depends entirely on the child's level of maturity and responsibility
- ☑ There are some positives to children using social media in a safe and controlled environment, such as self-expression, interaction and a monitored introduction to being a responsible Internet user

3

How to Talk to your Child in their Language

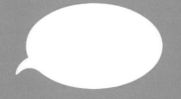

Kids today are natives of the digital eco-system, leaving parents feeling like trespassers – tiptoeing around their world.

> "The first hurdle to overcome is that you are speaking about a world that you have a limited understanding of"

If this sounds familiar, then it is time to make yourself at home in their world, by learning how to speak their language and actively mediate through digital stumbling blocks such as cyberbullying.

For many parents, the first hurdle to overcome is that you are speaking about a world that you have a limited understanding of and that you are not familiar with. You can feel awkward and clumsy trying to engage with your child if the associated language feels alien and you do not fully understand it.

The best way of overcoming this is familiarising yourself with the platforms, sites and apps frequented used by your child and adopting some of the lingo. Familiarising does not necessarily mean becoming a tech whiz on the site or platform in question, but a basic understanding of what the site does and some of the associated terminology will be useful. Our Three Step Guide below will help you to speak your child's digital lingo and be in a position to have confidence when speaking to them about their Internet adventures.

Three Steps to Speaking Your Child's Digital Lingo:

Step 1: Know what social media channels and digital outlets your child is using (Instagram, Snapchat, Skype, Viber, YouTube...the list goes on!). Simply find out by asking your child to show you the icons on their device and talk you through the name of each app. Your child may also be accessing social media and digital outlets through websites. Take a look through the history section on the browser of the laptop or the PC your child has access to – this will show you what websites they have recently visited.

Step 2: Download these apps on your own device, and visit the sites and games they play online. Try out these channels and outlets for yourself – play around and see what they are all about. Keep in mind that if you are setting up profiles, you should ask permission in the real world before sending your child a friend request in the virtual world. It is common that children do not wish to be connected with their parents online. If your child would rather not be connected with you, it is often best to respect their online space (once they give you some visibility of their account in another way, such as their password so you can take a look at the account or running through their account with you).

Step 3: Once you feel comfortable using these channels, you are far better equipped to talk to your kids in a way that they will really understand. You will have picked up some of the associated lingo just by browsing the sites or apps, and will

feel more confident once you truly understand what the various terms mean (See Glossary Page 214). If you are having some trouble with navigating the site or app, ask your child to show you around. Most kids are delighted to show off their digital knowledge and skills, and to help educate you in a world they are more familiar with.

If you are struggling with using the lingo in normal conversation, or with introducing it into your daily chats, try some of the examples we include below; the key is to keep it natural and sound somewhat knowledgeable, without being invasive or forceful – encourage your child to engage.

Examples of Questions to Ask

Instagram: Did you favourite anything today? Did you follow anyone new today?

Snapchat: What was your best 'snap' today? Did you make a 'story' today on Snapchat – what was it about? Did you save or 'screenshot' any 'snaps'?

Online gaming: What is your favourite online game? Who do you play with? Is that a friend from school or a virtual friend? Is he/she a big gamer? (We will have more on online gaming in Chapter 6; 'Hopscotch to Headsets')

Chat Apps: What app are you guys using to group chat - WhatsApp or Viber? Do you prefer those group chats or one-on-ones? Does your group send any photos?

For issues speaking with your child, recruit a digital champion to help

Top Tip

Two of the most popular channels for kids are Instagram and Snapchat. Instagram is a photo sharing app, which children use to share their pictures and videos, and to chat to one another both publically and privately. They can also follow celebrities and brands, and like other users' photos and videos.

Snapchat is also a photo and video sharing app. However it is different in that the photo disappears after a few seconds. This app is built for sharing with friends only, but there is a new function called 'Discover' which shows advertising 'snaps' that disappears after 10 seconds. Messages sent and received also disappear within 10 seconds, and users can build a 'story' over the course of a day with photos and 10 second videos, which can be seen for 24 hours by all of their friends.

Real Friends = Virtual Friends

Remember, the golden rule to online child safely is that real friends = virtual friends. The key to keeping your child safe online is to ensure that the people that they are interacting with online are also known to them in real life (friends and family).

Active Mediation

At Zeeko we believe education is the key to protecting our children online. Our mantra is 'to help parents and teachers to empower their children to protect themselves online through education'. This can be done through active mediation.

We do not let our children cross the road, we teach our children to cross the road. Similarly, we should not let our children onto the internet, we should teach our children how to use the internet.

Active mediation is about using the challenges we encounter with our children's internet usage as learning opportunities. This will ensure our children will learn how to behave responsibly online and to protect themselves online. Parents know their children the best. It is for parents to decide when to reduce restrictive mediation and when to start actively mediating.

It can be tempting to place a blanket ban on Internet usage for your child as a means of protecting them (restrictive mediation), but the negative impact of not developing digital literacy skills and missing the positive Internet experiences must be considered. They are also much less likely to confide in you about their digital experiences, and many kids will simply go underground with their Internet usage, using it behind their parent's backs in friend's houses and so forth. This actually opens them up to a much more serious risk, as they will be very reluctant to approach you should they run into difficulty, given that they have been online without permission. Active mediation involves working with your child and having open conversations to monitor their Internet usage and behaviour, and ultimately steering them towards responsible Internet usage without being overly forceful.

> *"It is important to have these regular conversations to ensure you are monitoring your child's relationship with the Internet"*

52   Zeeko Internet Safety Guide

It is important to have these regular conversations to ensure you are monitoring your child's relationship with the Internet. By speaking with children about their digital experiences, you are allowing them the opportunity to open up to you about their online world. Show your kids that you are interested in speaking their language and understanding their world. When they allow you into their online world, you can understand their feelings towards it and identify any potential issues or threats. Are they happy when they talk about these apps? Do they show any anxiety? Are they very secretive?

Three Key Steps to Active Mediation

Step 1: Familiarise yourself with the lingo associated with their preferred apps and games, as we mentioned earlier. Your child is far more likely to confide in you if they feel it is a topic that you have some knowledge of, and that they will not need to keep explaining the terminology to you.

Step 2: Adopt a **'Tell No Blame'** policy. If your child is fearful of punishment, judgement or scolding for confiding in you something that they have done online, they are unlikely to be comfortable to do so. Even if they have done something wrong, you should explain to them why what they have done is wrong, and help them come up with a way to fix it. If it is a genuine mistake and the first time they have done such a thing, it may be best not to punish them, as many kids feel guilty and anxious enough about the wrongdoing. If you do impose a punishment, it should relate to the action they are being punished for so that the consequence relates to the action — a punishment that is unrelated to what they have done with no explanation as to what was wrong will simply breed resentment and confusion. If they understand why they were wrong, and you have helped them rectify a genuine mistake, then it has been a learning opportunity and they will regard you as an approachable ally rather than an enemy.

Step 3: When your child comes to you with an online problem, take it offline immediately. Give a sense of acceptance by explaining to them that they have done the right thing by telling you. Next, ask them to talk you through the problem. Once you understand the problem take the virtual problem into the real world. If your child is following the golden rule, they will be only connected with their real friends. If it is a case of cyberbullying the key is to speak to a teacher at school or the parent of the bully to resolve the problem in the real world. If it is a 'virtual friend', block the user from your child's profile, revisit the child's privacy settings, and delete and block any other 'virtual friends'.

Who can be a Chatbudi?

We created the concept of a Chatbudi in order to get children to actively medicate with a trusted adult. We recommend that a parent should be their child's Chatbudi. However, this is not always possible. As an alternative a Chatbudi could be an adult who the child trusts, for example an older brother or sister; an aunt or uncle; a teacher, or a grandparent.

Consistently when we talk to parents at seminars they say their children are far more efficient at using apps, online games, social network sites and websites. Parents have a sense of helplessness when it comes to parenting online. Children maybe more efficient users of the internet but they do not have the maturity to make informed decisions about how to behave online. We know from our research that children use a large number of different apps, games, social network sites and websites. In one primary school surveyed with 245 pupils, the children were using 145 different apps, online games, social network sites and websites. Parents by definition have limited free time. It would be very difficult for any person to have a full understanding of all the different apps, online games, social network sites and websites that children use. It is not necessary to be a tech whiz to be a Chatbudi. This guide will get you up to speed with what you need to know. In addition, it is quick and easy to find additional information by doing an online search.

KEY TAKEAWAYS

- ☑ Familiarize yourself with the sites and apps your child visits
- ☑ Adopt active mediation — have open honest conversations to engage your child
- ☑ 'Tell, No Blame' — use family Internet issues as learning opportunities

4

The Virtual

School Yard Bully

Cyberbullying, at its simplest, is when one child targets another child with humiliating, embarrassing or threatening behaviour through the Internet or a mobile device.

For many parents, the primary concern is their child being the victim of cyberbullying, but the potential for your child to cyberbully is more prevalent than you might think. For many kids, cyberbullying can be unintentional, or the result of impulsive behaviour driven by emotions, and it is more common than most would assume. In many groups that we have worked with as part of our research, the majority of kids have displayed anxiety or remorse over some of their previous digital behaviour towards another individual more so than concern over how they have been treated online. This chapter will deal with not only how to manage your child being a cyberbullying victim, but also, to address your child engaging in cyberbullying behaviour.

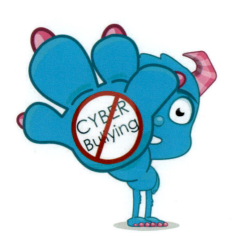

Zeeko has visited classrooms across Ireland to speak to children about what cyberbullying means to them. When we ask the kids have they heard of cyberbullying, hands shoot up in the air. However, when the children are asked to tell us what a cyberbully is, sometimes they are not entirely clear.

The truth is that the definition of a cyberbully is not as clear-cut as one might be led to believe. Cyberbullying comes in many shapes and forms. In order to help children better understand cyberbullying, Zeeko has created cyberbully personas to help parents and children alike to recognise the fine line between normal behaviour and bullying. Here are three common examples that we see most often:

The Accidental Cyberbully

Many children participate in cyberbullying without even being aware that they're doing it. Although a child may not generate abusive content, if they like, share or comment on it publically, they are partaking in cyberbullying behaviour.

A common form of accidental cyberbullying is exclusion. It can be difficult to determine whether an incident falls under normal exclusion or exclusion constituting accidental cyberbullying because the line is so indistinct. By not inviting another child to a party, the child hosting the party could be excluding them because they are not a close friend, and yet the child excluded can be very upset at being left out and seeing it all over social media. However, if the child hosting the party excludes a friend by cropping them out of a photo from the party – the child may not set out to cyberbully with intent, but can still engage in cyberbullying behaviour.

The problem is that exclusion can be hurtful to the child left out, and when the occasion is documented online through posts, photos, videos and Snapchats, this exclusion can be all the more hurtful given its public nature. The ubiquitous nature of the Internet means that the child can't help but be reminded of the exclusion, regardless of whether it constitutes cyberbullying or not.

Another form of accidental cyberbullying is when a child posts embarrassing content concerning another child, and is often in the form of a photograph. They may not see the harm in posting a 'funny' photo of another child, but the other child may be embarrassed by the photo and not want it publically posted. It is important that every child asks the permission of another child if they wish to post a photo of them, and does not disclose information online about another child without their permission. This includes tagging them in statuses, posts and check-ins.

60   *Zeeko Internet Safety Guide*

The Angry Cyberbully

For many children, social media and other online forums can present the ideal opportunity to vent their anger or frustration at a real world situation. For example, posting an embarrassing photo or a screen shot of a conversation online, because they are jealous, frustrated or annoyed. These children are acting impulsively on their emotions, without thinking through the repercussions. It is important to prevent your child from becoming a cyberbully by highlighting to them the potential aftermath of upsetting a friend through a digital platform, caused by acting on impulse.

Educate your child by explaining that once you upload content on the internet it is there permanently. They can say sorry but they can never remove it; anyone could have it saved, forwarded, shared or screenshotted, even if your child themselves has deleted it very soon after posting it. We use a simple rule to get this message across - it's called the t-shirt rule; if you wouldn't print it on a t-shirt and wear it around for your friends, family and teachers to see forever, do not post it online

In serious circumstances, the authorities can become involved to have the content removed, so it is important to stress that point if your child finds themselves at the centre of a serious incident. However, it can take a long time for the authorities to enforce removal requests, and if the content has spread across a number of jurisdictions, it can be very difficult to have the content removed from each source before it has spread to a new source.

This type of emotional cyberbullying can be a vicious circle; the victim may not know why they are being targeted and in their anger, they can retaliate and strike back, in turn becoming the bully. It's important to monitor your child's emotions when talking about the internet and online communication as most children will give some indication of negative emotions if they are embroiled in an online issue.

The Real Cyberbully

This is the cyberbully that engages in antisocial behaviour online out of boredom, malice or for their entertainment. It is often the most damaging form of bullying and the least detectable.

An example of this which we have come across on a few occasions is a child setting up a false persona online of another child in their class and using it to chat to other children, spreading rumours and posting embarrassing content. This phenomenon is known as catfishing and is wrong at best but extremely vicious and damaging at worst.

It can be the trickiest form of cyberbullying to tackle, because it may affect your child in the offline world – they do not need access to the Internet to be a victim. The bully may be speaking about them online or even pretending to be them online when the victim themselves has no online presence, and so, may not even be aware of what is going on for some time.

The best advice here is to regularly search the Internet for your child, which will usually show up their digital footprint and give some indication as to whether they are displaying negative or antisocial behaviour online. Do not jump to conclusions that they are lying if they tell you that any suspicious or harmful behaviour is not them. Investigate further and contact the cyberbully's guardians directly to resolve the issue. If you discover a false persona of your child online – report it and make the child's school, clubs and social groups aware. Get your friends and family on board too, to report the persona to the social network in question (e.g. Instagram or Facebook etc.) to have it removed swiftly - there is strength in numbers. Finally reassure your child that they are not in trouble of any kind, and that you are there to protect and support them.

This type of bullying can also involve a cyberbully setting up a fake profile and using this to attack victims, or it can be a child using their own profile posting nasty comments on another child's profile, photos, posts etc. It is extremely isolating for the victim; again it is so important to speak to your child about their feelings towards being online.

How to Deal with Cyberbullying

When it comes to online safety in general, whether your child is the target of unwanted communication or has become embroiled in a situation that they aren't comfortable in, it is vital that they are equipped with the tools to deal with it. It is very important to teach your child to remove themselves from any online situation which is making them feel uncomfortable or that they know they shouldn't be involved in. What can they do when they find themselves in such a position? Often, the first response can be panic, and they can become secretive, withdrawn and anxious. It may be the case that they aren't allowed on the website on which the incident has occurred, that they weren't supposed to be online at the time, or that they have posted something that they are ashamed of. Giving your child specific steps to take when such situations occur will empower them to take control of the situation, and to seek help from a responsible adult.

We champion the '**Stop Block Tell**' rule, as it gives the child definitive steps to manage negative digital experiences, to remove the sense of helplessness and panic, and to involve their Chatbudi as part of the solution. Explaining this rule to your child, and that they can call upon it if they ever run into trouble online, will help them to feel well-equipped for their online journey as well as communicating openly if an issue does arise.

STOP

Whether it is unwanted/uninvited contact from a stranger, a nasty post directed at or about them or a response to a nasty comment posted by your child, when they find themselves in a negative situation, they need to STOP.

So what do we mean by STOP? Do not respond to the comment or post. It can be difficult for kids not to retaliate or defend themselves and become embroiled in a vicious circle. Reinforce the idea that responding, even to tell the other party to "Go away" or "Leave me alone!" engages and prolongs the communication, and the other party is quite likely to respond in turn. So STOP any communication with the other party immediately.

BLOCK

Almost all social media platforms, online games and websites have the facility to block a user. This will mean that they can no longer contact your child. Familiarise yourself with this function on any sites or platforms used by your child, so you can help them with this step. Depending on the severity of the inappropriate conduct, you may wish to report them to the site/platform administrators, which you can also do.

With all of this said, it is important to stress to your child that these functions are there to protect them from negative or harmful contact, and shouldn't be used as weapons against real life friends in the event of a small bust-up. We have heard many stories of kids blocking and reporting one another over minor arguments, which are soon resolved. Using these digital weapons of blocking and reporting can lead to their friend's profile being removed by site administrators, which of course is appropriate in the face of bullying or persistent unsolicited contact from a stranger, but not so appropriate for a friend with whom they will have resolved whatever issue has arisen in a short space of time.

Below, we'll explain to you how to block other users on the most popular platforms amongst kids; Facebook, Instagram, Snapchat, WhatsApp and Viber.

Snapchat

- From the main profile screen, click **'Added Me'**

- Click the User name

- Click the **'Gear'** icon
- Press **'Block'**, which will prevent that person sending any Snaps or viewing the Stories of the account from which you are blocking them
- You can also remove them from your friends list by clicking on their name and choosing **'Remove Friend'**

When you block someone on Snapchat, their name will remain on the friend list of the profile you've blocked them from, but that profile/username will no longer appear on their friend list. This means they cannot message the account from which they are blocked, so they may notice that you no longer appear on their friend list.

Instagram

You can only block and report using the app version of Instagram. As with a lot of the Instagram functions, the blocking and reporting functions do not work on the desktop version.

The user blocked will not be notified of the blocking, and your identity will not be shared with the user you report.

- Go to the profile of the user that you wish to block/report
- Click ••• (iOS), ⋮ (Android) or ••• (Windows), depending on your device type
    - Select **'Block User'** or **'Report'**

Facebook

There are a few different ways to block and report people on Facebook, but this is the simplest. The blocked user will not be notified of the blocking. If a user is reported, they will not be notified of the identity of the reporter.

- Go to the user's profile
- Click ⋯ on the profile (to the right of the screen)
- Select **'Block'** or **'Report'**

WhatsApp

When a user is blocked on **WhatsApp**, they are not notified. However, they may notice that they no longer see the **'Last Active'** information in the chat screen and messages sent to the contact that has blocked them has one check mark beside it rather than two. In addition any calls attempted by the blocked party will not connect.

There are a few ways of blocking someone on **WhatsApp**, which differ slightly depending on the device used.

iPhone

- If the individual is not in the users address book, there is an option at the top of the chat screen to **'Block'**. For the first message from an unknown contact, use the option to **'Report Spam and Block'**

- Otherwise, go to the **'Settings'** menu:
    - Select **'Account'**

    - Select **'Privacy'**

o   Select **'Blocked'**

o   Click **'Add New'**

o   Select the contact to block

Android:

- If it is the first message from an unknown contact, there is an option to **'Report Spam'** and **'Block'**

- Otherwise, from the **'Chats'** screen:
    - Tap the **'Menu'** button on the device. For most devices the Menu button is a physical button on the phone and it is not part of the screen. The button will appear different on different phones. See example below.

The Virtual School Yard Bully   75

o   Select **'Settings'**

o   Select **'Account'**

- Select **'Privacy'**

- Select **'Blocked Contacts'**

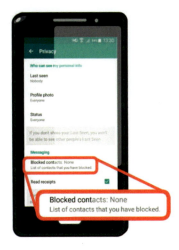

- Click ➕👤 **'Add Blocked Contacts'** symbol in the top right

- Select the contact you wish to block from the list

Viber

When a user is blocked on Viber, they will receive no notification of the blocking. They will be able to continue sending messages to the blocker. However, the blocker will not receive those messages.

The blocking procedure differs slightly depending on the device type.

iPhone & Android

- If it is the first message from an unknown contact, there are 2 options at the top of the screen; **'Add'** or **'Block'**

- A user can also be blocked from a group chat (but the block will only affect one-to-one communications):
    - Swipe left from the group screen
    - Select the contact to be blocked
    - Select the device menu
    - Select **'Block'**
- If the user to be blocked is already in the contact list
    - For iPhone, from within the conversation info screen
        - Select the gear icon
        - Select **'Block'**

- For Android from within the conversation info screen
  - Swipe the screen left
  - Select the device menu
  - Select **'Block'**

TELL

This is a really important step in managing a negative online experience; TELL your Chatbudi. We encourage children to find a Chatbudi; someone they know that is close to them, who can help them to stay safe in their exciting digital journey. This individual should be over 18 year old and a person your child can trust. Whether you are their chosen Chatbudi or they have chosen someone else, they should tell their Chatbudi immediately if something online is concerning or upsetting them. The Chatbudi can help them stop the abuse if they have not managed to do so already, to take more serious steps if necessary (i.e. to report to the site administrator, or to report to the authorities, depending on the severity of the situation) and ultimately, to reassure the child that they are there to help them and to protect them. It is important to reiterate to the child that they are not at fault if they have been the victim of cyberbullying, as many victims can hold themselves accountable. If it is the case that they have accidentally cyberbullied or engaged in emotional cyberbullying, and the situation has escalated, help them understand why they shouldn't have done it and how to rectify the situation. The blame game can actually hinder the child coming forward and being honest in future, so helping them come to terms with what they have done and why it was wrong, as opposed to pointing the finger and judging the child, is usually best practice. If there is a punishment, it should relate to their wrongdoing, to reinforce their understanding of why what they did was wrong and that it has direct consequences. Unrelated punishments with no explanation surrounding why their actions were inappropriate usually breeds resentment and confusion in the child, and there is no real learning for them about why their behaviour was wrong.

Many children become quite upset and withdrawn when they are faced with negative online experiences, and their self-esteem can be shaken. Therefore, it is important

that they discuss how the incident made them feel, that they understand they are not being blamed and that they realise there is help for them to manage this situation.

Introducing the **'Stop Block Tell'** Rule into your home will ensure your child is equipped with the steps to take in order to deal with any negative digital experiences that they may face. Making it the norm within your home, similar to the Safe Cross Code will normalise it for your child, and reassure them that these are the logical and widely-accepted steps to take should they find themselves in challenging digital situations.

Bystanders

It is important to be aware of the role of bystanders. Research on cyberbullying is increasingly finding that bystanders have a powerful role, and can have an effect on the situation and the reaction of the victim. It is important to encourage your child not to be a passive bystander or one that implicitly supports a bully when they witness cyberbullying occurring.

Frequently Asked Questions

What do I do when a child tells me they are a victim of cyberbullying?

Your child opening up is half the battle in solving a cyberbullying case. Firstly, praise your child for telling you and assure them that they will not get into any trouble. Ask your child to show you the cyberbullying evidence; if it is a child that you know take the problem offline and into the real world immediately by speaking to their parents or teachers. If it is a person or child that you do not know ensure that they are blocked from your child's profile, check your child's safety settings and if necessary, report the bully or abuser to the site administrators. Take the opportunity to educate your child on the importance of keeping their social media profiles private, only accepting real world friends and not speaking to strangers

How can I tell if my child is a victim of cyberbullying?

Symptoms of a child being cyberbullied are very similar to traditional 'school yard bullying' i.e. low self-esteem, nightmares, avoiding school, changing routine and presenting signs of anxiety. However, the physical act of bullying is not there (although that is not to say that there is not a crossover between the two in many instances). The act of cyberbullying cannot be heard like name calling in a school yard, or seen through cuts and bruises. A cyberbully is a silent bully and just like traditional 'school yard bullying' the victim is likely to stay silent too. For this reason it is important to ask children about their social media experience and feelings.

My child won't talk to me about their experience online – how can I keep them safe?

If you do not succeed at first with talking with your child, recruit a digital champion to help. This can be a babysitter, older cousin or sibling who can speak to them regularly and help monitor their safety. We encourage children to find a Chatbudi; someone they know that is close to them, who can help them to stay safe in their exciting digital journey. A Chatbudi should be over 18 year old and a person your child can trust. Their relationship with their Chatbudi is a two way street. Children can educate their Chatbudi on how to use a mobile phone, apps and the Internet, and the Chatbudi listens to the child and monitors the emotions they express about their online activity. This builds on the concept of active mediation and engagement, rather than dictating and restricting.

> *"Find a Chatbudi. Someone they know that is close to them, who can help them, stay safe in their exciting digital journey"*

How do I know if my child is a cyberbully?

We have seen that in a lot of cyberbullying cases, it is accidental or emotional. In such cases, it is normally resolvable. When we speak to children who have engaged in such behaviour, they tell us about the anxiety and regret that they experience afterwards. A simple question to ask is, "Have you ever done something online that you regretted?" It is also a good idea to review your child's digital activity with them, and if you spot something that may be accidental or angry cyberbullying, ask "How would your friend feel when they see that? If your child is involved in 'real cyberbullying' it can be difficult to detect. It is likely that this child has been involved with a fake profile and secretive behaviour. If you are suspicious that they may be engaging in this type of cyberbullying, they are unlikely to admit to it when asked. It may be necessary to look through their Internet history, or ask them to show you around their profile (with no warning so they do not have the opportunity to delete or hide any of their harmful or nasty behaviour).

What can I do if my child is a cyberbully?

If you have detected that your child has been involved in accidental or angry cyberbullying behaviour, assure them that although they made a mistake it is possible to make it better in the real world. However, it will remain permanently in the online world, and you should treat this as an opportunity to reinforce that point of the 'stickability' of the Internet. You should empower them to rekindle damaged friendships or hurt feelings by apologising in the real world to the person they have abused. If your child is actively cyberbullying in a 'real' way it can be slightly trickier to detect and resolve. Encourage open conversations about their online identity and behaviour, and speak to them about the consequences of their actions –

encourage empathy for the way they have made someone else feel. We find it very effective to ask, "How would you feel if someone did that to your little brother/sister or to your cousin, or to your best friend?" Most seem to empathise more with the thought of someone hurting those close to them, than to the thought of being on the receiving end themselves.

KEY TAKEAWAYS

- ☑ Cyberbullying can be unintentional – understand how your child's online behaviour may impact others and communicate this to them
- ☑ Discourage your child from taking anger out online; open up the lines of communication so they talk to you instead – be a Chatbudi!
- ☑ Create open conversations with children to detect negative emotions towards the internet – these negative emotions can indicate issues online, whether they are the victim or the unintentional bully

5
Stranger Danger

"Do not talk to strangers" - a social norm accepted by children everywhere. Everywhere, except online.

A surprisingly high amount of primary school children in Ireland are interacting with strangers online. The following are the percentages that have ever spoken with a stranger online, or played against or with a stranger online: 17% of 1st class; 23% of 2nd class; 38% of 3rd class, 42% of 4th class, 46% of 5th class, and 54% of 6th class[5]. This is as a result of their multi-functional digital world – they are chatting, gaming and social networking.

Safety rules are second nature to children; belt up in the car, look left and right crossing the road and do not talk to strangers. So why in an age where our children are so aware of the dangers of speaking to strangers in the real world, are so many comfortable with interacting and engaging with strangers online?

The issue stems from the fact that children suffer from a cognitive disconnection between the real world and the virtual world. They often do not transfer real world rules such as 'Stranger Danger' and protecting their personal information into the virtual world. Children do not comprehend the importance of these rules as they often cannot see the real life danger attached to their digital activity. This naivety can leave children exposed to the threat of unwanted interaction with strangers online.

---

[5] Source: Zeeko All Ireland Digital Trend Report

As parents, it is our role to ensure that our children are protected online, and a huge part of this is ensuring that rules which apply in real life are being transferred into their virtual world.

Children are growing up with technology as an integral part of their lives. As we have reiterated a number of times in this book, it is such a positive tool that will support a wide range of life skills for them, from personal and academic skills through to their professional lives. Technology and the Internet will become more and more a fundamental part of your child's life as they grow and develop.

This chapter is designed to help you equip your child with the knowledge and tools to apply 'Stranger Danger' rules online and to protect them from this digital danger. A brief overview of our research on children's interaction with strangers online will be covered, before we look at the key threats that parents need to be aware of. Finally, this chapter will conclude with some simple steps that you can take to minimise the risks to your child's safety.

Digital Stranger Danger Threats

The Zeeko Academy is our programme where we host seminars and workshops for schools, teachers, parents and education organisations. In the Zeeko Academy we have a module called Digital Stranger Danger. This development is following on from recent concern over the 'Talking Angela' app. We spoke to many anxious parents who experienced their children talking into their phone at an animated cat - speaking about their school life, home life, family and friends. The natural reaction for any parent is immediate panic that their child is talking to a stranger. Although this app may indeed be harmless, it is not safe practice for children to share any information online.

We also spoke to children about their thoughts and feelings about this app. Many of them played regularly and loved it; they saw no harm in sharing their personal details. We related this to real life and asked if they would tell a stranger on the street the same information. Immediately their attitude and demeanour changed, as they looked incredulous and quoted 'Stranger Danger'.

We have conducted extensive research on children's internet habits to understand when children are exposed to the risks of Digital Stranger Danger. There are two key threats we need to be aware of as parents to help us protect our children.

Threat 1: Unwanted Communication via Online Gaming

Children usually first become exposed to the risk of Digital Stranger Danger when they play online games. They typically begin to play games online (such as Minecraft, Subway Surfers or Crossy Road) from around the age of 7. They often interact with their friends through a chat function or headset while gaming.

The risk is that your child can choose to chat with any online gamer, or they can be contacted by a fellow gamer. The growing incorporation of chat functions into games means that children are beginning to communicate online younger than ever before. 17% of 1st class primary school children reported that they are interacting with strangers online.[6]

---

[6] Source: Zeeko All Ireland Digital Trend Report

Threat 2: Unwanted Digital Stranger Following your Child's Social Media Activity

Children are further exposed to Digital Stranger Danger when they become active on social media. This can begin as young as 8 years old (3% of 2nd class students use Instagram or Snapchat). The most popular social media app among this age category is Instagram. As children build their social media profiles, they generate followers or friends. These are the other users that your child is connected with, and that can see your child's activity.

One of the primary risks here is 'catfish' profiles. These are fake profiles, sometimes created to attract children. These can be masquerading as the profile of a famous celebrity, or simply a fake profile set up pretending to be another child. When your child connects with a digital friend or follower, they are leaving their digital world open to be observed, so it is vital that your child connects only with those that they know in real life.

The first step as a parent is to understand the nature of your child's online habits in order to understand the associated threats. What sites are they visiting? What platforms are they using? Are they interacting with others online? Are they using the video technology on their device, or the audio technology, or maybe the headphones for their gaming device? Who are they chatting to? These are all questions you should consider to understand their online activity.

The second step is to introduce a few safety barriers to mitigate the threat. The most fundamental of these is instilling in your child the fact that interacting with strangers online is just as dangerous as speaking with a stranger in real life. But go further than just preaching to your child about 'Stranger Danger' – explain WHY it is dangerous, what the risks are and how it could impact them in real life. In addition, we recommend these other safety barriers that you can call upon to help you protect your child from Digital Stranger Danger, see below.

Digital Stranger Danger Safety Barriers

It is straightforward to prevent these threats in your child's digital life. Here are five steps you can take at home to safeguard against Digital Stranger Danger:

- Explain the dangers of speaking to strangers online to your child and emphasise that real world rules still apply online. Help them to understand why interacting with strangers online can be dangerous,

Stranger Danger 95

what the real world consequences can be and why they should stick with people they know in real life

- Screen your child's followers and friends on the social media and gaming sites that they use on a regular basis. Ensure they are real world friends. Work with your child to delete and block any followers and friends that they do not know

- For younger children you can set up 'play dates' for online games between your child and their real friends. Organise a time slot where you allow your child join an online gaming session. Outside of these organised times, do not allow your child to use a headset while gaming and turn off the chat function of their games

- Create a Digital Safety Contract between you and your child that allows them X amount of online gaming play dates if they follow X digital safety rules. If they break the set of rules the number of play dates can be reduced. It is important that your child feels a part of putting this contract together, and that it's agreed upon mutually. They will buy into it and feel a sense of personal responsibility to uphold the rules more so than a contract that is imposed upon them

- Teach your child to keep all personal information private. This means that their profile photo should not make them easily identifiable (for example, wearing their jersey from the local football club or their school uniform), that they do not mention their address or school in their descriptions and that they do not tag themselves in locations

Tweetable takeaways on Digital Stranger Danger

- ☑ 54% of 6th class children are interacting with strangers online
- ☑ Online gaming is the most common form of Digital Stranger interactions
- ☑ Stranger Danger can come in the form of social media followers and friends, as well as online gamers
- ☑ Children can communicate via games with strangers through chat functions and headsets

6

Hopscotch to Headsets

Online gaming has become somewhat of a phenomenon amongst younger generations, with children constantly discussing their gaming and individuals making careers out of blogging about the latest games and hacks (cheats for games).

Games' market research agency Newzoo reports that gaming generated $81.5 billion in revenue globally in 2014, which is double the revenue of the international film industry. So what is it about gaming that gets kids so excited?

The reality is that children are playing games for a whole array of reasons. From the entertainment factor to the cyclical sense of reward they experience, the vast majority of kids really enjoy gaming. However, although there are so many positive aspects, Dr Douglas Gentile, Director of the Media Research Lab at Iowa State University reports, "Almost one out of every ten youth gamers shows enough symptoms of damage to their school, family, and psychological functioning to merit serious concern."

Our research at NovaUCD has led us to identify four key threats when your child is playing online:

- Communication from a stranger
- Cyberbullying
- Exposure to inappropriate content
- Excessive internet use

While our previous chapters on Stranger Danger and Cyberbullying cover the first two problem areas, this chapter will concentrate how online gaming contributes to excessive internet use and inappropriate content. Then we will provide you with a review of two popular games (as highlighted by the Zeeko All Ireland Digital Trend Report) with children today, Minecraft and the Call of Duty series (CoD). Finally we will provide an overview of the Steam digital distribution platform. The chapter is designed to highlight the dangers associated with gaming and provide you with simple ways to address these issues.

Psychological Effects of Gaming

Dr Andrew K. Przybylski, a behavioural scientist at Oxford University conducted a study on psychosocial adjustment related to online gaming. He discovered that children who spend more than half their daily free time playing video games demonstrated more negative adjustment. This study tells us that anything over 2-3 hours per day of online gaming leads to lower levels of prosocial behaviour and life satisfaction. This in turn means that on average, children exposed to higher levels of online gaming are less satisfied in offline activities. Negative adjustment can damage your child's relationships, the development of their social skills and overall well-being, which is quite a frightening thought. The next chapter will discuss excessive internet use in more detail and help you identify the signs of excessive internet use.

Online Gaming – Exposure to Inappropriate Content

Inappropriate content is a very broad, umbrella term, as we will discuss in Chapter 10 *Inappropriate Content*. For many parents, exposure to inappropriate content is the primary concern associated with gaming. In gaming the two most common types of inappropriate content are violence and sexualised content. Violent and sexual content will be the focus of the remainder of this chapter. However inappropriate content does not have to be as extreme as violence and sexualised content; it can be a range of things which are not suitable for a child, and these will be outlined later in the book, in Chapter 10.

Violence typically comes in the form of warfare or shooter games such as Call of Duty (CoD), Ghost Recon and Halo. Sexualised games often come in the form of criminal activity oriented games such as Grand Theft Auto. In this game, the player can steal cars, get involved in police chases and solicit prostitutes.

Violence in video games is a concern for many parents. Some researchers feeling that there is little to no harm resulting from playing these games. Research in this area is complex and nuanced, with mixed findings.

We recommend that you prevent your child from being exposed to inappropriate content by allowing them to play age-appropriate games only. If your child is expressing interest in games such as Call of Duty or Grand Theft Auto, speak with them about why they enjoy that game and what aspect(s) of it that they like in particular. From our experience, children are not attracted to the inappropriate nature of violence or sexualised games. Generally, children are more attracted to the challenge and rewards attached to the game, they are drawn in by a particular element involved in that game. For example, many kids who play Grand Theft Auto enjoy the free-roaming aspect, whereby they can walk or drive around and explore. Explain why this game is inappropriate, and that you are not comfortable with them playing it. You can then find a child-friendly alternative as a compromise, which incorporates the element(s) that your child enjoys, in a more child-friendly way. In the case of Grand Theft Auto, The Simpsons Hit & Run is very similar in concept, without the adult content. Common Sense

Media (commonsensemedia.org) is a fantastic resource, which we recommend to source age-appropriate alternatives.

Game Reviews

We have taken two of the most popular games amongst the 8-12 year old group (as self-reported in our All Ireland Digital Trend Report) and reviewed them from a parent's perspective. Common Sense Media, which we mentioned above, have great reviews for most popular games, so it is worth glancing at their reviews before you purchase a game for your child.

Minecraft

Minecraft is a very popular game with children today, and consistently features as one of the most popular games amongst the 8-12 year old age category in our research. The game somewhat resembles Lego, in that users can build a virtual world from building blocks. It encourages creativity and employs the use of their imagination, so it can be very positive from a developmental perspective. However, as with most technologies, it is important that as parents, we are mindful of the functionality of the game and its suitability for our child.

Excessive internet use

The tendency to use Minecraft excessively differs from child to child. We see that children do not show signs of excessive internet use when playing this game in a controlled setting. This involves a limited or scheduled time on the app, which is routinely monitored and enforced where necessary.

Exposure to inappropriate content

There is very limited amount of inappropriate content in Minecraft. There are some cartoon-like characters, but they are age-appropriate.

Overall, we give Minecraft our Safety Seal of Approval on three conditions:

- Play as a single user
- Limit time spent on Minecraft to 1 hour maximum a day
- If playing in multi-user zone – set up 'play dates' for one supervised hour with real friends. If cyberbullying occurs, end the play date and take it offline to deal with the issue at hand.

Call of Duty

The age restrictions on Call of Duty (CoD) vary from version to version, but on average the age limit is 16 – 18. It is a first person shooter game whereby gamers can play alone or with other users through remotely connecting each other into the game; this can be friends or strangers. The game series centres around a warzone and the first few versions were set in World War II. Newer versions are modern warfare and future warzones.

Excessive Internet Use

In cases of excessive internet use, children are not necessarily consumed by the violence, but more so the sense of reward for completing levels. This sense of reward can be satisfied in age-appropriate alternative games, such as Minecraft.

Inappropriate content

Exposure to inappropriate content while playing Call of Duty is a real threat. The majority of the harmful content in a CoD game falls into the categories of violence and profane language (the majority of which comes from other users in online multiplayer mode). Users are expected to routinely perform violent acts such as shooting or deploying explosives, and are exposed to violent scenes. There is little to no inappropriate sexual content in this game, as can be seen in other games such as Grand Theft Auto, as discussed above.

CoD is not a suitable game for children. However, we are aware from speaking to other parents in the course of our work and our research that many children come into contact with this game while visiting a friend or relative's home. This can trigger a desire in your child to get their own copy of this game, or to play it again. The best way to address this is by speaking with your child about the content in the game, and why it is inappropriate, before agreeing on a suitable alternative, as outlined earlier in the chapter.

Steam

Steam is a digital distribution platform for PC games. The URL for the website is http://store.steampowered.com/. While lots of the games on here are great, and very educational, and appropriate for all ages, some are more suited to older audiences, but do not necessarily have a suggested age rating as the games are often independently developed. Therefore we recommend researching any games you are considering downloading from this platform.

KEY TAKEAWAYS

- ☑ Allow your children to play age appropriate games only
- ☑ No screen time an hour before bed, and ideally, no devices in the bedroom
- ☑ Turn the chat function off in every game to prevent communication from strangers, unless your child is engaging in an organised playdate with real world friends
- ☑ If your child is asking to play inappropriate games such as CoD or Grand Theft Auto, find an age-appropriate alternative using the Common Sense Media resource

7

Excessive Internet Use

Excessive Internet use may seem like a relatively new phenomenon, but it has in fact been an issue for over 20 years, with many psychologists devoting their entire careers to this area.

As we have stated throughout this book, the Internet is an incredibly powerful and positive tool, but excessive usage is exceptionally common in our society today. Smart devices and laptops have become so tightly integrated into our lives that we often feel lost without them. We rely heavily upon them in most aspects of our life from communication and social networking, to our schedule and banking. This chapter will discuss the symptoms of excessive internet use, the potential effects and offer some suggestions on how to tackle and prevent this condition in your child.

Spot the Signs of Excessive Internet Use

Being able to identify excessive internet use early on is crucial in tackling the condition. Dr Kimberly Young is a psychologist who has specialised in this area since 1995, and has pioneered the study of this condition. She has identified symptoms in children which are key indicators of a larger problem:

- Agitation and anger when interrupted online
- Irritable if not allowed online
- Loses track of time online
- Sacrifices sleep to spend time online
- Neglects fundamental parts of their daily lives to spend time online, such as homework, hobbies or chores
- Prefers to spend time online instead of with family and friends

If you spot these symptoms in your child, it is important to seek the help of a medical professional, who can refer the child on for specialist help if necessary. The common response towards excessive time online is to simply confiscate the device, either temporarily or indefinitely, but this can actually do more harm than good if the child has been spending a lot of time online. They will internalise negative feelings towards you as the parent, and you may be perceived as 'the enemy'. Withdrawal symptoms can also be extreme, causing anxiety, anger, irritability and depression. Instead of this knee-jerk and abrupt reaction, take a gradual approach; slowly withdraw the device by gradually reducing the time you will allow them to spend online. Discuss the negative consequences of spending so much time online, and suggest offline alternatives that you can both do together.

Causes

It is not known exactly what causes excessive internet use, but it is generally agreed upon by medical professionals that there is usually a predisposition towards excessive use in most cases. There have also been links drawn between other mental disorders such as anxiety and depression. In addition, there has been research into the link between extreme shyness; difficulty engaging and interacting with peers, and; excessive internet use.

Effects

Excessive internet use can affect different people in very different ways, but some of the more common effects amongst younger people include:

- Withdrawing from social situations and their social life (self-isolation)
- Difficulty communicating and interacting with family, friends and strangers in the real world
- Lower productivity and procrastination
- Physical symptoms, such as backache, headache, neck pain, vision issues and carpal tunnel syndrome
- Technostress – according to the Oberlin College of Computer Science, sufferers can internalise the manner in which technology works such as accelerated time and perfect results in tasks
- Anxiety and depression when not using a device
- Insomnia

Preventing Excessive Internet Use – The 5:1 Rule

We have conducted extensive research into excessive internet use, the habits amongst children in Ireland and the optimum time spent online in order to come up with an appropriate guideline in this regard. As a result, we are pioneering the 5:1 Rule; 5 hours of real world activities to 1 hour of 'screen time'.

The premise behind this guideline is very simple; medical and psychological professionals recommend 1-2 hours as the maximum time a child should spend using screens per day (most notably recommended by the American Academy of Paediatrics (AAP)). On average, a child spends 18 hours a day between sleeping, school, homework, meals, hygiene and chores, leaving 6 hours of 'free time'. With all of this in mind, we propose 5 hours spent on real world activities for every 1 hour of 'screen time' – the 5:1 Rule. Bear in mind that real world activities can include homework, meals etc. and they do not need to be supervised activities – it could simply be going out to play with friends in the front garden!

In order to use the 5:1 Rule, it is important to understand what we are referring to when we say 'screen time'; the time spent looking at a laptop, PC, TV, smartphone, tablet, iPod etc. All of these devices involve 'blue light' technology, to which children should not be overexposed. It causes suppression of the hormone, melatonin, which is also known as the 'sleep hormone'. Excessive exposure to this 'blue light' will disturb your child's sleep patterns. It is highly recommended that screens are turned off an hour before bedtime, and that there are no screens in the bedroom. Experts advise that 'blue light' exposure at or around bedtime impede upon sleep quality, and can have a significant impact on the child's learning capacity, by affecting memory consolidation (the process through which new information is committed to the brain). In other words, a good night's sleep is fundamental in optimising memory consolidation and learning (The American Physiological Society, 2013).

In addition, we recommend downloading a piece of software called f.lux (the app is currently available for Android devices). The programme is free to avail of, and removes the blue light from your screen in line with the natural sunset, thus mimicking natural sunlight patterns. This minimises the impact of 'screen time' after sunset upon melatonin production, which in turn reduces the impact of 'screen time' upon sleep patterns, so it is a valuable tool for children and adults alike.

KEY TAKEAWAYS

- ☑ Identifying the symptoms of excessive internet use in your child and tackling the issue early on is crucial
- ☑ Confiscating the device as a knee-jerk reaction can do more harm than good – gradually withdrawing the device will allow the child to effectively adjust
- ☑ Introduce the 5:1 Rule in your home, to give your child a guideline as to how much 'screen time' is allowed
- ☑ 'Blue light' technology suppresses melatonin production, which can impede sleep patterns, and in turn will negatively impact memory consolidation

8

Safety Settings

As parents, it is our duty to protect our kids online as they learn to become responsible digital citizens. However, that is easier said than done. With ubiquitous access to digital channels, various multiple devices, our kids have never been more connected. While it is impossible to be there 24/7, through education, conversation and putting in place a few safeguard settings, you can dramatically reduce the risk posed by the Internet.

When we speak about safety settings, one of the main points we make is that while they are an excellent tool to have in place, they are by no means a substitute for education and conversation. There is no safety setting or safety software that we have come across which is 100% effective. They are there to complement what you teach your child about Internet safety, and to reduce the risk of serious harm. We like to think of them as online training wheels; while they will not prevent a fall, they will reduce the risk of a fall substantially and improve the chance of staying upright dramatically.

Safety settings tend to fall into 6 broad categories:

- Internet providers and access
- Mobile phone providers
- Websites
- Search engines
- Safety programmes and apps
- Devices

Items 1 to 5 will be covered in this chapter. Devices will be covered in Chapter 9. We go into more detail across a wide range of options during our Parent Crash Courses, which you can find out more about on **www.zeeko.ie**, but this chapter will focus on the most popular options.

Internet Providers and Access

Most providers actually do offer parental controls or safety settings, although many do not publicise it or make it well-known to customers. These controls vary from provider to provider, from restricting Wi-Fi access times by device, to restricting the content accessible from certain devices. The likes of Sky, Eircom, Vodafone (in Ireland and UK) and AT&T (in the US) offer this as part of their service, although with some providers a small additional fee may apply.

As well as offering parental controls as part of their own service, Irish provider Digiweb offer a modem (Fritzbox 7360) which will work with other broadband providers, and allows you to control when children/ or persons within the household use the broadband and which devices can connect wirelessly to the internet. You can also create lists of words/ terms and websites that your children are not able to search or access. If you are not a Digiweb customer, this modem costs around €150, either as a once off payment or as a small upfront fee followed by monthly instalments. It is well worth speaking to your current broadband provider and other local providers to find out what parental controls or safety settings that they can offer.

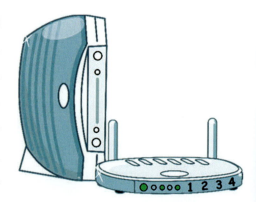

Ikydz

Just plug this device into your router, turn it on and take control of the Internet in your home, from anywhere in the world. With ikydz you can control how long a gaming device is allowed to be played, when Facebook or Snapchat can be accessed, when smartphones or smart TV's can be on. Ikydz controls every internet dependent device in the home. It can block certain sites – pornography, gambling, self-harm sites – and the list of blocked sites are updated every day by Ikydz. There is an interesting feature called **'Meal Time'** which allows you to remotely shut off Wi-Fi access for all the devices in your home with one single press of a button on the Ikydz mobile app.

Mobile Phone Providers

When it comes to mobile phone providers, the ICIA (Irish Cellular Industry Association) Code of Practice has been developed by the major mobile phone companies in Ireland and provides for parents' visibility of their child's mobile phone usage and the services they access. This means that when a valid request is put to the operator, the parent should have access to the child's mobile phone account, subject to all applicable data protection and privacy laws. Essentially, this means that both the parent and child have access to the records held by the mobile operator regarding the child's account including numbers called, account balances and the services available on the child's mobile phone. You will usually have to set up dual access with the operator in order to access this information, but that is relatively easy. Although the Code of Practice also recommends the offering of capabilities for parents to customise access to content by children using their mobile device, this does not appear to be a widespread reality at present.

When buying your child's first mobile phone, it is worth shopping around between providers, to see what they can offer in terms of parental controls and safety settings. Most networks have initiatives or apps in this domain; for example, in Ireland, Vodafone have **Safety Net** and eMobile and Meteor

have **SafeSurf**. Some of these services are not compatible with certain devices though, so ensure to double-check before you purchase (e.g. **Safety Net** is only compatible with Android devices at present). If your child already has a device and is on a particular network, make sure to liaise with the operator to see what they can offer you with regards to safety and parental controls.

Websites

When it comes to website safety settings, YouTube is by far the most commonly used site amongst kids, so we will use this as our example here. However, other websites that your child uses may also have safety settings, so it is worth looking into before your child uses the site.

If you are accessing YouTube from a desktop or laptop, simply follow these instructions:

1) Scroll to the bottom of the page and click '**Restricted Mode'**

2) Select **'On'**

3) Click **'Lock Restricted Mode on this browser'** and enter your Google/Gmail credentials. This means that only those with your password can change these settings, and again, we recommend that you keep this private from your children

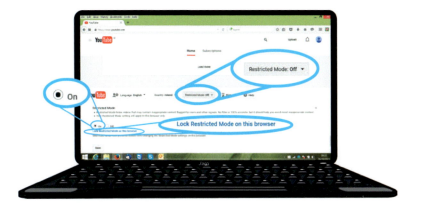

4) Bear in mind that this makes these settings applicable only to the browser on which you set them (e.g. if you were using **Google Chrome** when you applied the settings, then they apply only to **Google Chrome**). You will need to set up the settings on each browser if there is more than one used on the computer in question

Search Engines

When your child is searching online, it is a good idea to either restrict the search options on Google, or depending on their age, to use a more child-friendly search engine. While it is not realistic to expect search engine safety settings to be 100% effective (there are means of getting around filtering with encryption etc.), they are certainly safer than a search engine with no filtering or safety settings. Google **SafeSearch** will block a lot of inappropriate content and images (although again, it is not 100% effective), and is very easy to switch on by following the steps below:

1) Click on **'Settings'**, in the bottom right hand corner of your screen

2) Select **'Search Settings'**

3) Select '**Turn on SafeSearch**'

4) Click '**Lock SafeSearch**'. This is a very important step as it ensures the settings stay in place and prevents other users from turning off SafeSearch unless they have the log-in credentials (you require a Google/Gmail account for this). Make sure to keep these details to yourself – your children should not know the password, and should have to ask you to enter the password for them if they ever require it!

Safety Settings 129

There are a number of child-friendly search engines available, which aim to filter content, and are geared at younger children. These include **Google Kids, Google Junior, Safe Search Kids** and **KidRex**. Having tested these search engines, we would recommend **KidRex** as the best option. Again, they are not 100% effective, and some allow through some inappropriate content during our testing or display advertising, but **KidRex** came out on top for us, as among other reasons, it had (a) no adverts, and (b) child friendly search results. You can set this as the default search engine for your child if you wish, so that this is the search engine that pops up when they open the browser window (**Internet Explorer, Chrome** or **Mozilla Firefox**).

Safety Programmes and Apps

There are a huge amount of software packages and apps on the market operating in the online child safety and parental control domains, some of which are relatively pricey. While, like all of the other safety settings we have discussed in this chapter, they are not 100% effective, some will offer the additional protection and features that you are looking for above and beyond what we have discussed thus far.

There are many programmes available for laptops and desktops, and it is important to do your research to find the package which best suits your needs. While many are paid, or offer freemium options, there are some free options too. The most popular and highest rated programmes (both paid and free) amongst tech safety experts include **Net Nanny, K9 Web Protection, Naomi and Spyrix**, which all offer different features. Many of these features will overlap with what you already have available to you between your Internet provider, your mobile phone provider, search engine and website settings and device settings, so doing your research will ensure you are actually getting additional features, which are not available to you otherwise.

When it comes to apps, there is a plethora available, so it can be difficult to decipher what is effective and reputable. **Mobicip**, **K9 Web Protection**, **Browser for Kids Lite** and **Ranger Browser** are some of the more popular titles, and similar to the software mentioned above, some are paid and some are free.

For Android users in particular (see Chapter 9), there may be a need to use an app for further protection for the child. Apps like **AppLock** let you password-protect certain apps without locking down access to the entire device. **Kid Mode** and **Kids Place** allow children to play their favourite Android games, read stories and paint pictures, without the risk of accidentally buying something on the device, deleting emails or accessing other apps. **Mobile Fence** protects children from accessing inappropriate content (websites, apps, videos) through smart devices, as well as limiting usage time to combat excessive internet use. Also, parents can monitor their children's location in real time and are notified when their children enter or leaves a safety zone set by their parents. There is a range of similar apps available in the Play Store, as well as in the App Store for iOS users.

Zeeko Safe Communication App

We are developing an app to safely introduce children to online communication. The app is based on feedback from parents and teachers that we have met during our seminars around Ireland. It aims to alleviate the online risks we speak about in this book: cyberbullying; excessive internet use; digital stranger danger, and inappropriate content. The app allows parents to approve every single connection their child has and oversee every single message their child sends and receives. Parents can set the times their children can access the app. Also, there is a concise report on their activity. The app is available on the App and Google Play Stores.

KEY TAKEAWAYS

- ☑ No safety setting or parental control tool is 100% effective
- ☑ There are a multitude of low cost or free tools available from operators and providers, so there really is no reason not to use them
- ☑ Research what is available to you – oftentimes it is not well-publicised what your mobile operator or broadband provider can offer you as part of the service
- ☑ If you decide to invest in further programs or tools to help keep your child safe, review your family's needs and research available products before making a purchase

9

Devices

The important thing to note when it comes to devices is that safety settings vary quite widely by device, and often, between different versions of the same device. This book is looking at the most popular devices, but we run through these in far more detail and across a wider range of devices in a workshop setting during our Parent's Crash Course (see **www.zeeko.ie** for more information on these courses). Firstly, we will look at **iOS**. The second section deals with **Android**. The third section addresses **Windows**, and the fourth sections looks at the **Apple Mac**.

iOS

The first devices we will explore are the **iOS** devices; **iPhone**; **iPad** and **iPod Touch**. The safety settings for all of these devices are set-up the exact same way, so follow the steps below.

Restriction Set-Up

1) From the Home screen, select **'Settings'**, then **'General'** from the menu that appears

2) Select **'Restrictions'**

3) Click **'Enable Restrictions'**

4) Set a password, which you will use to change your settings or turn off **'Restrictions'** in the future. Ensure this password is different to the password used to access the phone. This will prevent your child accessing **'Restrictions'** if they have the password to access the phone

Features and Apps Set-Up

Now you can customise safety settings for (1) Features and Apps (2) Content (3) Privacy (4) Allow Changes, and (5) Game Center. We offer our recommendations on these settings below. There are a total of 37 items you can customise in **'Restrictions'**. The numbered items in the list correspond to the numbered items in the pictures.

1) Disallow **'Safari'** if you are uncomfortable with your child accessing the Internet

2) Many kids like taking photos, so it is ok to leave the **'Camera'** on, once you have given your child some guidelines around sharing images

3) If your child communicates with faraway family or friends, you may wish to leave **'FaceTime'** on for video calling

4) **'Siri'** is essentially voice control, or an **'interactive assistant'** on the device. Some kids like to use it for the novelty factor. You can change the settings later in the menu to disable **Siri** using explicit language or accessing web content as part of the search

5) **'AirDrop'** is a means of transferring files wirelessly between devices, but is seldom used and could be switched off

6) **'CarPlay'** allows the device to interact with in-car displays and systems, so for most children, this should be turned off

7) You can remove **'iTunes Store'**, **'iBooks Store'**, **'Podcasts'** from the Home screen

8) You can choose to disable **'Installing Apps'**

9) You can choose to disable **'Deleting Apps'** and **'In-App Purchases'**

Devices 141

Content Set-Up

Next, you can choose what content settings you are happy to allow. Again, our recommendations are below:

10) Click on **'Ratings For'** and choose Ireland (leave it as the US if you wish, it is not too dissimilar)

11) **'Music and Podcasts'** should be switched off **'Explicit'**

12) **'Films'** set to **'G'** (General) and **'PG'** (Parental Guidance) or set not to allow movies

13) **'TV Shows'** set to **'GA'** (General Audience) and **'Ch'** (Children) (**'YA'** Young Adult, **'PS'** Parental Supervision , **'MA'** Mature Audience)

14) **'Books'** – disable explicit sexual content

15) Select the appropriate **'Apps'** rating for your child, bearing in mind their age and maturity

16) Disable **Siri's** explicit language and web search content features

17) **'Websites'** – either limit adult content or enter specific websites only

18) Set require password to **'Immediately'** which means that apps cannot be purchased without your password (particularly important if you want to disable the ability to install apps)

142   Zeeko Internet Safety Guide

Privacy Set-Up

Next you can customise your privacy settings:

19) With **'Location Services'**, we recommend selecting **'Don't allow changes'** so that new apps are prevented from using location services, and turn off **'Location Settings'**. Your kids generally should not need GPS functionality

   a) Turn off **'Share my Location'**

   b) If you leave **'Location Services'** on, check what apps and features use **'Location Settings'**. Make the appropriate changes as you see fit

20) In **'Contacts'**, select **'Don't Allow Changes'**, which means that new apps cannot access your contact lists and check what apps do have access to your contacts

21) Do not allow changes to **'Calendars'**

22) As above, do not allow change to **'Reminders'**

23) Again, we would recommend not allowing changes in terms of **'Photos'**, so no new apps can use your photos and check what apps have access to photos

24) With **'Share My Location'** select **'Don't Allow Changes'**

25) **'Bluetooth Sharing'** – do not allow, your child should not need to share items via Bluetooth

144   *Zeeko Internet Safety Guide*

26) **'Microphone'** – we would recommend not to allow. As we have discussed earlier in this guide, voice communication via apps should be limited to those apps you know, so monitor what apps are able to access the microphone and make sure the child cannot add new apps to the list without first checking the app.

27) Some social media sites will request access to your other social media accounts/apps, but again disabling is best

28) **'Advertising'** – do not allow changes

Allow Changes Set-Up

29) **'Accounts'** – do not allow changes

30) **'Mobile Data Use'** – do not allow changes

31) **'Background App Refresh'** – do not allow changes

32) **'Volume Limit'** – whatever you see fit

Game Center Set-Up

33) Disable **'Multiplayer Games'**

34) Disable **'Adding Friends'** on **Game Center**

When you have Restrictions on, you might notice that you are missing a particular app or feature, that you cannot use it or that the icon on your main menu is dimmed. If it is something you need, you can just change your Restrictions

Family Sharing Set-Up

If you are an all-Apple household, you can use the new **'Family Sharing'** features of iOS 8 to manage everyone's devices.

1) Go into **'Settings'** on your iPhone or iPad and open **'iCloud'** (if you need instructions for setting up iCloud, you will find them on Apple's support site)

2) Select **'Set Up Family Sharing'** and tap **'Get Started'**. You will have to click through a bunch of screens to verify that you are the family organizer and that the correct credit information is on file at the iTunes Store

3) To add an account you want to manage, select **'Add Family Member'**, enter their iCloud email address, and then tap **'Next'** (you may be prompted to sign in with your Apple ID if you have not already)

4) This new family member will receive a notification on their phone asking them to accept the invitation to Family Sharing and to agree to share their iTunes purchases (**'Ask to Buy'** feature for those under 18) and location information (can be changed from iCloud settings)

5) You can also share apps with other family members and have a shared family calendar etc.

Android

Android does not actually have extensive parental controls or restrictions on phones like iOS devices, but between the settings you can use and some apps you can download, you can still protect your device. They do have slightly better features on their tablets, which we will run through below. But features for controlling **Play Store** purchases work on most Android phones and tablets so these instructions apply for both. Bear in mind that settings can vary slightly by device, and so they may not follow exactly as below:

1) Open the **Play Store** app (sign in with your email address and password if you are not already logged in)

2) Press the **'Options'** button (usually located either in the top left hand corner of the screen or below the screen) and select **'Settings'**

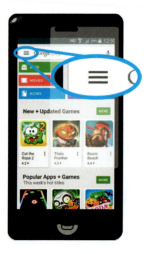 

3) Scroll down to the **'User Controls'** and select **'Parental Controls'**

4) Turn **'Parental Controls'** on

5) It will then prompt you to set and confirm a PIN

6) Under **'Apps & Games'** and **'Movies'**, select your chosen rating by age (usually done by PEGI standards (Pan European Game Information))

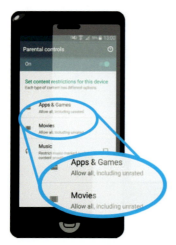 

7) With **'Music'**, **'Parental Controls'** restricts music purchases from the Play Store. Explicit songs in **'Radio'** can be blocked in the Play Music app settings

8) Ensure that **'Require authentication for purchases'** is checked on the menu (some versions can still download free apps)

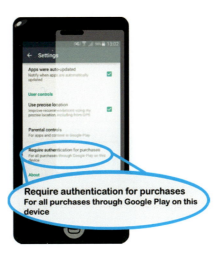

9) Lastly, On the main Settings menu (accessible from your Home screen) scroll down to Security and ensure the option to allow installation of apps from other sources is disabled

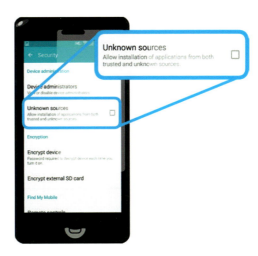

Android devices can vary quite a bit, so the above may not be entirely accurate for your version. However, it is usually relatively similar and there is a **'Parent Guide to Google Play'** available online. If there is quite a bit of variation for your handset, and you cannot apply the settings, you should refer to the manufacturer's literature or to your phone provider for further guidance

> *You can enable flight mode to restrict web, call and messaging features, but it is very easy to turn off, so it is not a reliable solution*

For Android tablets running **Jelly Bean 4.3** or later, you can actually have multiple profiles with the option of restricted profiles (4.2 allowed multiple profiles) which effectively turns the tablet into a family device. So basically, you as the device administrator control the app permissions of each user profile, and so you can control what your child is accessing.

1) From the tablet Home Screen, go to the app menu and select **'Settings'**

2) Scroll down to the **'Device'** section, and then select **'Add User or Profile'**

3) Select **'Restricted Profile'**

4) If you do not already have screen lock enabled on your device, you will need to do it now. Choose **'Set Lock'** and choose your PIN, pattern or password

5) There should be a settings icon next to the new profile, so press the icon to give the profile a new name

6) A list of all the apps you have installed on the device will now show up. The default setting is that a restricted profile cannot access any of the apps, so you can go through the list and choose which apps you are happy to allow access to and select those

7) Now, from the lock screen, your account is password, PIN or pattern protected, while your child can access their own account with only the apps you have selected available. Although the Google Play Store icon will still appear on the screen, they will get a notification that they do not have permission to use the Google Play Store if they try to access it

Windows

When it comes to Windows computers, you can set up parental controls, although the means of doing so varies between versions of Windows. Below are the instructions for the most recent versions of Windows, but Windows 7 users can go to **'Control Panel'** and under the **'User Accounts and Family Safety'** heading, select **'Add or Remove User Accounts'.** Proceed to set up a standard user account and follow the steps onscreen until you are prompted to login or set up an account for the Windows Live Family Safety website. Once you have logged in and gone to the website, you can follow step 18 onwards.

We recommend having a separate user profile for your child/children if the laptop or PC is used by other members of the family (for example for work or by a teenager) as the safety settings will need to be different, and what is suitable for your child may impede your use of the device.

Windows 8:

1) From the pop-up menu at the right hand side of the screen, click **'Settings'** and select **'PC Settings'**

2) Then choose **'Change PC Settings'**

3) Select **'Accounts'**

4) Select **'Other Accounts'** from the menu

5) Click **'Add an account'**

6) Select **'Add a child's account'** and click **'Next'**

7) You will have the option to enter an email address for your child if they have one, to sign up for a new email address for them, or to **add an account with no email address**. An account with no email address simply means that they will need your assistance to download apps from the Windows Store. Here, we have opted to create an account without an email address. Click **'Next'**

8) Enter the user details for the child for which you are creating the account and click **'Next'**

Devices 165

9) Click **'Finish'**

10) The **'Manage other accounts'** screen will appear again, and you can then choose to set up the controls you wish to put in place. Select **'Edit'** on the account you want to work with

11) Ensure **'Account type'** is set to child and click **'OK'**

12) Then, in **'Control Panel'**, under **'User Accounts and Family Safety'**, select **'Set up Family Safety for any user'**

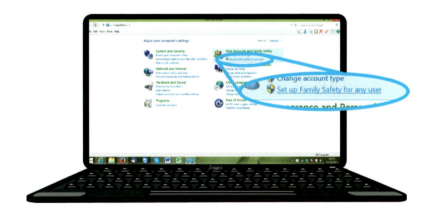

13) Select the account that you wish to manage settings for, and click **'Manage settings on the Family Safety website'**

14) You will be redirected to the Microsoft Account homepage, where you will need to sign in if you have a Microsoft account already, or create an account if you do not have an account

Windows 10:

10) Select **'Settings'** from your computer's main menu

11) Select **'Accounts'**

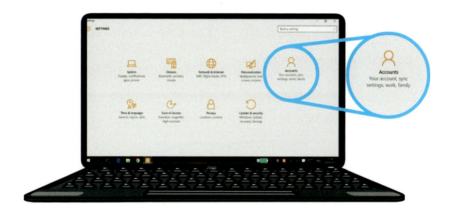

12) Select **'Family and Other Users'** from this menu

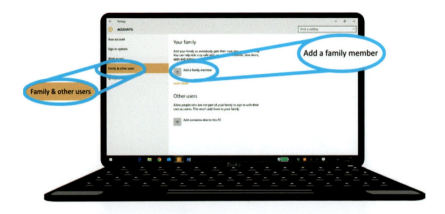

13) You will need to sign in using your Microsoft account, or create one if you do not have one already

14) Then you can add your child (make sure to select the **'Add a Child'** option, and enter their details (just click the option at the bottom if they do not have an email address)

15) Continue through the dialogue boxes, entering the required information

16) In the **'See What's Relevant to Them'** dialogue box, ensure to unselect the **'Enhance their online experiences by letting Microsoft Advertising use their account information'**

17) Their account will then be created and you will be brought back to the main dialogue box, where you click **'Manage Family Settings Online'**

All Windows users:

18) The Microsoft Account webpage will then appear, on the **'Family'** tab. Click on the child's profile that you want to update

19) A dashboard then shows up – you can customise all safety settings from this page

20) The first section is **'Recent Activity'**. From here, you can make sure you have reports set up if you want them, and can select to have them emailed to you directly each week

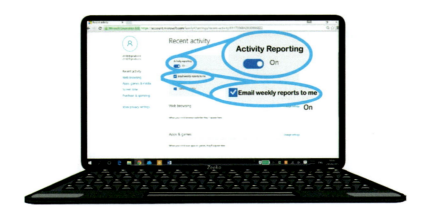

21) Clicking on the **'Web Browsing'** section, you can turn on the **'Block Inappropriate Website Function'**, and turn on the function to only allow certain websites if you wish (particularly for younger kids). You can add these websites at the bottom, and block the sites you do not want your child visiting. When the **Parental Controls** block access to a game or program, a notification is displayed that the program has been blocked. Your child can click a link in the notification to request permission for access to that game or program. You can allow access by entering your account information

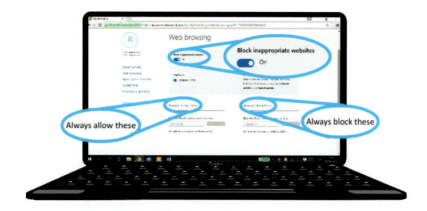

22) In the **'Apps & Games'** section, you can block inappropriate apps and games on the device. Bear in mind that these are games which are ON the computer itself, not online games. You can set it for a particular age rating and then further customise what to always allow and what to always block as you wish

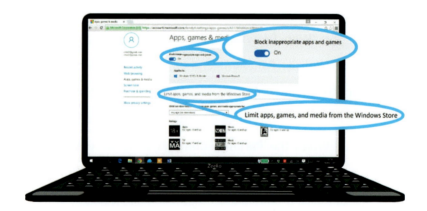

23) The **'Screen Time'** section allows you to limit your child's time online by day, so that they cannot access the web before a certain time, or after a certain time on specific days

Apple Mac

Mac laptops and desktops have quite comprehensive safety settings, which can be activated by following the instructions below. This section will show you how to **Create a User** and to customise **Parental Controls** for, **Apps, Web, People, Time Limits** and **Other.**

Create a User

1) From the Apple menu, choose **'System Preferences'**

2) We would recommend having a separate user account for each child so you can customise the settings accordingly. If you do not have separate user accounts set up already, choose **'Users & Groups'**

3) First **'Click the lock to make changes'** and then enter the administrator's name and password, and click **'Unlock'**

4) Below the list of accounts click on the **'Plus' (+)** button

5) From the **'New Account'** pop-up menu select **'Managed with Parental Controls'**. Fill in the remaining fields with full name, account name, password, password verification, and, optionally, a password hint. Click **'Create User'**, and the controlled account is created

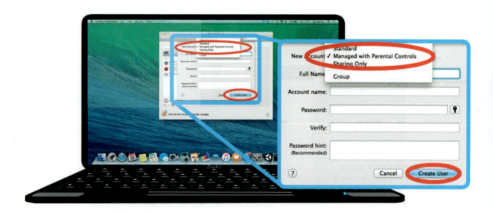

178   Zeeko Internet Safety Guide

Set Parental Controls

1) To begin configuring the account, in the **'Users & Groups'** window click the **'Open Parental Controls'**

2) Select the user account on the left side of the window that you would like to enable filtering for[7]

---

[7] Note: Parental Controls cannot be enabled for administrator accounts (admin accounts will not appear in the window). You can check 'Accounts Preferences' in 'System Preferences' to see which account(s) have what level of access (Admin, Managed, and so forth)

Apps

1) Click the **'App'** tab

2) If your child is not familiar with using a laptop, and if you want to make the desktop simple, select **'Use Simple Finder'**. Only three folders reside in the **'Simple Finder'** version of the Dock (My Applications, Documents, and Shared). Meanwhile, the only applications your child can see are those you have designated by selecting the **'Only Allow Selected Applications'** option. Dock modification is categorically disallowed in **'Simple Finder'**

3) Then select **'Limit Applications'**, and decide the age rating you are happy with in terms of the app store rating

4) You can also select **'Allowed Apps'**, and search the items you are happy for your child to access, such as **'Game Center'**

Web

1) Choose one of the three modes under **'Website Restrictions'**. The three modes are: **unrestricted**, **automatic**, and **whitelist**

2) With unrestricted, when **'Allow unrestricted access to websites'** is selected, the Internet content filter logs websites that the account visits but does not restrict web browsing. Visited websites are still logged and can be examined in the **'Logs'** tab of **'Parental Controls'** preferences

3) When **'Try to limit access to adult websites automatically'** is selected, the Internet content filter does its best to block websites with inappropriate content. To do this, the filter uses the same technology that the Mail application uses to identify **'junk'** mail. The Internet content filter will attempt to identify whether a web page is safe or not by examining various properties of the website including text and structure.

4) Additionally, the Internet content filter will block a website if the website identifies itself as adult-oriented using the **RTA** (Restricted to Adults) (http://www.rtalabel.org/) rating system or alternatively the **SafeSurf** (http://www.safesurf.com/ssplan.htm) rating system, as well as forcing **'safe'** searches with some search engines. So you are essentially relying on the rating system and filtering system here, to keep inappropriate content out

5) In this mode, the Internet content filter logs all visited and blocked websites, and flags them as such in the **'Logs'** tab of **'Parental Controls'** preferences

6) In certain situations, the automatic Internet content filter may mistakenly block a safe website or allow an adult-oriented website. For example, if the website uses an uncommon language or if there is very little text on the page. These websites can be identified in the **'Log'** tab of the **'Parental Controls'** preference pane and added to the **'Always Allow'** or the **'Never Allow'** lists. These lists can also be accessed by clicking the **'Customize...'** button. Websites that are mistakenly blocked can also be allowed by clicking the **'Allow...'** button on the blocked web page and authenticating as an admin user

7) If **'Allow access to only these websites'** is selected in **'Parental Controls'**, the Internet content filter blocks any website which is not on the list. When the blocking web page is presented, a list of allowed websites is

also shown. If using Safari, allowed websites are displayed in the bookmarks bar

8) In whitelist mode, visited and blocked websites are flagged in the **'Logs'** tab of **'Parental Controls'** preferences and can be added or removed from the whitelist there

Https note: For websites that use SSL (secure sockets layer) encryption (the URL will usually begin with https), the Internet content filter is unable to examine the encrypted content of the page. For this reason, encrypted websites must be explicitly allowed using the **Always Allow** list. Encrypted websites that are not on the **Always Allow** list will be blocked by the automatic Internet content filter, regardless of the suitability of their content

Note: For most websites, the Internet content filter considers the domain name and not the path. For example, if http://www.example.com is added to the list, then http://pictures.example.com will be allowed, as will http://www.example.com/movies

People

1) You can choose whether to allow your child join multiplayer games on **'Game Center'**, and whether they can add friends on **'Game Center'**. You can choose to **'Limit Mail to Allowed Contacts'**, and also to receive an e-mail permission request should your child attempt to communicate with someone who is not on the **'OK'** list. Lastly, you can **'Limit Messages to**

Allowed Contacts', and then in the bottom of the dialogue box, you can add the contacts you are happy to allow your child to communicate with

Time Limits

1) This allows you to establish weekday and weekend time restrictions. You can limit the hours per day that can be spent on the computer, and you can prevent access to the Mac when it is time for bed, choosing different times on school nights and weekends. Your child will get a fair warning shortly before shut down time so that they can save work, close down games and wrap up what they are doing. They can also request more time, which needs to be approved by the system administrator (i.e. by you)

Other

1) Here you can disable certain features, such as the Built-in Camera, Dictation, Printer Privileges, CD/DVD burning and hide profanity in Dictionary

Logs

1) This is where you monitor your child's online behaviour. Select **'Logs'** from the bottom right

2) You can see the web sites they have visited (or the attempted visits), the applications used, and who they chatted with. You can log activity for one week, one month, and three months and so on. You can also group logs by contact or date

Do not forget to click the lock at the bottom of the screen again to lock the settings you have just put in place!

Is your child using another Mac in the house? You can remotely manage parental controls across all the Macs in your home network. You will have to set up an administrator account across all the computers you want to manage. In the lower-left corner of the Parental Controls window, click the small gear icon (just above the padlock). From the pop-up menu, select **'Allow Remote Setup'**. *Repeat this exercise on each Mac you want to manage*

KEY TAKEAWAYS

- ☑ Safety setting are not a substitute for education and conversations with your child

- ☑ Most devices have safety settings. Before you purchase research what various devices offer to ensure they meet your needs

- ☑ Children should have separate accounts on devices where possible, to enable you to have safety settings in place without restricting your own usage or compromising your files or data

- ☑ We advise against allowing devices in bedrooms less than one hour before bedtime. This will reduce the blue light from interfering with your child's sleep and also help to avoid the temptation to go online after lights out

10

Inappropriate Content

When we speak with parents, exposure to inappropriate content often features in the top 3 concerns regarding their child spending time online.

And yet, when we visit schools, this is often the least explored topic, with many children unsure of what the problem with exposure to inappropriate content really is. Many do not understand why seeing photos of their favourite celebrity scantily clad or playing a gory and violent video game may not be what is best for them.

For many parents, this is a topic that can be incredibly difficult to get to grips with. It can be particularly daunting, given the wide range and masses of content at your child's fingertips when they are online. This chapter will break it down for you – from what inappropriate content actually means, to how to easily and effectively manage this risk within your home.

What is Inappropriate Content?

Inappropriate content is often used as an umbrella term to cover a range of topics deemed unsuitable for children. But there is no short answer when it comes to what constitutes inappropriate content, as it depends on the parent, as well as the maturity and age of the child in question.

We at Zeeko would consider the list below to be inappropriate content for most parents and children:

- pornographic material or content depicting nudity
- content containing swearing, inappropriate or offensive language
- content promoting alcohol and drugs
- sites that incite or encourage inappropriate or harmful behaviour such as vandalism, crime, terrorism, racism, eating disorders and even suicide
- pictures, videos or games which contain or promote violence or cruelty to other people or animals
- gambling sites
- unmoderated chatrooms (no one monitoring the conversation, language used or content shared)

This issue for many parents is that there are so many ways (both accidental and intentional) that your child can end up viewing inappropriate content, which include:

- Child stumbling across inappropriate content through a keyword that they do not realise has 2 meanings
- Child searching for a keyword relating to inappropriate content out of curiosity
- Child stumbling across inappropriate content on a website or app that they use (advertising, pop-ups, links, mentions)
- Child is sent links to inappropriate content by friends
- Child clicking on a spam message which redirects to inappropriate content

It seems to be a general assumption that most children fall under one of two polar opposite ends of the spectrum when it comes to inappropriate content; they are either oblivious to the existence of such content, or that they are purposefully seeking out such content. The EU Kids Online Survey[8] which was conducted in 2013 appears to dispel that myth - 58% of kids surveyed said they worry about coming across pornographic, violent or other unsuitable content.

Violence and pornographic material tend to be the biggest concerns amongst parents. As we have covered violence in some level of detail as part of Chapter 6, we will focus more so on pornographic content in this chapter. Pornography tends still to be somewhat of a taboo topic; so understandably, some parents are anxious or unsure as to how to approach the topic with their children.

Pornographic Content

Our children are living in a highly sexualised world nowadays, with sexual images bombarding them both on- and offline. From advertising to social media sites, sexualisation is prevalent in modern society. A new wave of celebrities such as Rihanna, Miley Cyrus, Kylie Jenner and Kim Kardashian often post sexualised photos on social media where they are followed by many young children. Children are becoming curious or more exposed to sexuality and sexualisation at a much younger age.

---

[8] EU Kids Online (Feb 2013), study of 10,000 children

While it may be assumed that pornography and sexual content is a topic that features for teenagers rather than children, a number of studies conducted in the past few years suggest otherwise. In fact, in an ICM (public opinion research agency) survey for the BBC in 2014, a quarter of the kids surveyed said they had seen online pornography by the age of 12. Of those, 78% had stumbled across it accidentally, meaning that the vast majority of children do not seek out pornography in the first instance. Looking specifically at Irish statistics, 21% of 9-16 year olds reported seeing sexual images on or offline according to the Net Children Go Mobile Report in 2014, it is no longer traditional mass media that is the most common source. It is actually social networking sites, which in turn means that children are more exposed than ever to this content and at a younger age than ever.

10% of 12-13 year olds fear that they are addicted to pornography

A statistic that we at Zeeko found particularly alarming comes from an NSPCC and Childline survey conducted in the UK in 2015, which reported that 10% of 12-13 year olds fear that they are addicted to pornography. So out of the 700 12-13 year olds surveyed as part of that group of 2000, 70 said they felt addicted to pornography , which to most of us is pretty startling.

While viewing pornography is often considered part and parcel of growing up, of adolescent curiosity and of exploring their sexuality, the age at which children are being exposed to such content is younger and younger. The

Internet has made pornography readily accessible and easy to stumble upon, regardless of the user's age. While viewing pornography at a young age is, of course, a huge concern for most parents, it is the susceptibility towards addiction that is the primary worry. Viewing pornography can be a compulsive behaviour, and because of the pleasure and reward cycle associated with it, it can be difficult to break the habit, much like with gambling or substance abuse. It is the potential for repetitive viewing of pornography to negatively shape the child's view of what a 'normal' relationship is, to impact on their perception of genders, and other core areas of everyday life and relationships.

The good news is that compulsive viewing and addiction are not issues that affect the majority of kids when it comes to pornography. Pornography is less likely to become an issue for you and your child, if:

- You are equipped with the tools to address the topic
- It is something that your child understands is inappropriate for their age and that pornography does not reflect real world relationships or dynamics

Tackling Inappropriate Content

Although we have focused on pornography up to this point, these tips for tackling inappropriate content are applicable for all forms of inappropriate content, and will help you to address these matters in your family:

- Safety settings will help in protecting your child from inappropriate content but **will not prevent it altogether**
- The goal is to empower your child to avoid inappropriate content themselves by equipping them with some basic rules (such as do not open emails from addresses they do not recognise, or do not click on pop-ups), and to know what to do if they encounter inappropriate content
- Start with a chat about inappropriate content – that there are things they may come across on the Internet that they would prefer not to see and that you would prefer they did not see, and why

- Have age-appropriate conversations

- For example, with pornography, that it does not depict real people, or normal loving relationships, or with violence that you can seriously injure or even kill people by acting that way and the repercussions etc.
- This can be a good time to mention that the media (celebrities, advertisers, TV, magazines etc.) can impact how we feel about ourselves, or what we think is 'normal behaviour'
- Agree on the sites and apps that are best for your child to use, based on what they like to do online
- Reinforce the idea that your child can talk to you, or their Chatbudi about anything they come across online that makes them uncomfortable
- Give them specific steps to take if they do come across images that make them feel uncomfortable (e.g. put the iPad face down, and go and speak to their Chatbudi about what they have seen)
- Do not panic if your child comes to you having seen something inappropriate - reassure them that they have done the right thing by coming to you

- With teens and older children, it is important to communicate that some types of inappropriate content can have serious repercussions for them. For example, watching content promoting or inciting terrorism can get them into trouble with the law, and that certain types of pornography are illegal, meaning watching it can have serious consequences, such as impacting a future working with children
- If you believe your child may be addicted to pornography (if they are watching it compulsively, if it is beginning to affect them in other areas of their life, if it seems to be skewing their view of relationships and sex etc.), then you should seek the assistance of a medical professional. They will be able to properly assess the situation and refer you on for specialist help if necessary

KEY TAKEAWAYS

- ☑ Conversation is the key when it comes to inappropriate content – speak to your child early on about the types of inappropriate content that they may come across and explain <u>why</u> it is inappropriate

- ☑ Empower your child to recognise potential threats when it comes to inappropriate content

- ☑ Equip your child with specific steps to take if they come across inappropriate content (e.g. flip the iPad over face down and speak with their Chatbudi about what they have seen)

- ☑ Do not openly panic, regardless of what your child tells you – this will cause them to panic, to retreat into themselves or to internalise that the topic they were broaching is a taboo subject that should not be discussed

11

The Resource

Hub

i

Keeping our children safe online is a priority for most of us, and thankfully, there are some fantastic resources to help us do so. We have mentioned a few of these throughout this book, but this chapter will round up our top picks when it comes to useful resources for parents and teachers.

Zeeko

www.zeeko.ie

We publish a weekly blogs and tips with the most up-to-date information in this domain, so it is worth subscribing to receive these into your inbox automatically. Our cutting edge and hands-on research means that we are at the forefront when it comes to Internet Safety for kids, and we endeavour to make that information publically available as soon as possible (subject to the appropriate data privacy protocol), to help other parents stay up to date with the latest trends. We also often address individual concerns or suggestions for topics on our blog or social media platforms (anonymously if you wish), so if you have a particular concern or query, you can contact us via our website.

Common Sense Media

www.commonsensemedia.org

Common Sense Media is a US-based website that has a wealth of information and tools for parents and teachers alike. One of our favourite resources on the site is the 'Reviews' tab, whereby you can read other parents' reviews of games, movies, TV shows, apps, websites, music and books. They have an extensive database, and each review scores games in terms of the positive and negative aspects they contain too (e.g. positive role models, consumerism, drinking, drugs and smoking etc.). One of the most useful features of this tab is that they offer suggestions for age-appropriate alternatives to most games, so if your child is particularly attached to an inappropriate game, this will point you in the direction of a similar but child-friendly alternative to appease them.

In addition, Common Sense Media offer their top picks when it comes to games, movies, apps etc., as well as extensive resources on a broad range of relevant topics for parents. Lastly, they have a 'Parent Concerns' tab, which is a mixture of blogs and articles from professionals as well as interaction from other parents.

Internet Matters

www.internetmatters.org

Internet Matters is a UK-based not-for-profit organisation, which has some fantastic resources for parents and teachers. They work with a number of closely aligned organisations such as the UK Safer Internet Centre and Ofcom to promote online safety. Their 'Issues' section gives a great overview of the primary concerns arising from Internet usage, such as cyberbullying, online grooming and sexting, while their 'Advice' section offers some useful guidance for parents on the various devices, apps, social networks and offers age-specific advice. Some of the 'Controls' section advice is only applicable to the UK, but the device instructions are generally accurate and similar to our guidance in Chapter 9.

Insafe

www.saferinternet.org

Insafe is a European network of national awareness centres of EU member states, as well as a handful of non-member states (Iceland, Norway, Russia and Serbia). Its goal is to empower children and young people to use the internet, as well as other online and mobile technologies, positively, safely and effectively, and to promote shared responsibility. Safer Internet Day is the brainchild of Insafe, and is marked internationally with an awareness campaign and events. It's worth having a look at the website for an overview of what work is being done on an international level.

Webwise

www.webwise.ie

Webwise is the Irish Internet Safety Awareness Centre, funded by the Department of Education and Skills and the EU Safer Internet Programme. They are members of the above mentioned Insafe network, and are part of the Professional Development Service for Teachers (PDST). The website has in-depth explainer videos for parents, covering social media platforms, apps, safety settings etc. as well as some great teacher resources, such as anti-bullying kits and handbooks.

Safer Internet Day

www.saferinternetday.ie

This website is dedicated to Safer Internet Day in Ireland, which usually falls in early February. There are a few downloads for parents, including a Family e-Safety Kit, some in-class exercises including videos for teachers and competitions for children too. Around Safer Internet Day, you can have your event listed on the website if you are organising something associated with Internet Safety.

12

Endnotes

When Zeeko began, we were driven by a desire to help protect children from the dangers and risks that they faced online through technology. Very quickly, we realised that technology would only form a minor part of the solution, and that education was an integral part of promoting Internet Safety. In the words of Nelson Mandela, "Education is the most powerful weapon which you can use to change the world". Our aim is to empower children, parents and teachers with the knowledge they need to be responsible Internet users and guardians, and to make the Internet a safer place for children to explore.

So, we immersed ourselves in our research, conducting focus groups, interviews, and surveys, and reading endless reports from other researchers. We want to understand the trends in technology usage and the potential issues before they even happen, we want to be in a position to forewarn parents of online threats and equip them with the tools they need to protect their children before the problem even occurs.

This guide is a summary of our cutting edge research and findings so far, and is designed to get parents and teachers up to speed, regardless of your digital proficiency. It will enable you to get to grips with your child's digital world, and put in place the safeguards to protect your child from digital threats. The less you feel like an imposter in your child's cyber adventure, the more you will be able to encourage open communication with them on all things digital, whether they are positive or negative. They key is that you want your child to feel comfortable to come to you, or their Chatbudi, should anything, or anyone bother them online. That will only happen when you feel comfortable yourself in discussing the topic.

The common thread throughout this guide is that conversation is key. There is no substitute for dialogue, for discussing with your child what they are seeing online, what is being said online, what the appropriate conduct is and equipping them with the tools to deal with negative situations that they may encounter while online. While there are various safety settings, parental controls, apps and pieces of software available on the market, these complement conversation; they are not a replacement.

The advent of handheld technology has brought with it many possibilities, but also, it has brought many risks and challenges. Children now can have 'anytime, anywhere' Internet access and communication. While many of the uses are entirely positive, there are negative connotations also, and we as parents and educators must tackle these issues to protect our children.

Lastly, if you take away one thing from this guide, we hope it will be that the Internet is not a negative tool. It is a very powerful tool that can have negative impacts when the correct safeguards are not in place, and when the user is not equipped to deal with the potential threats. The Internet plays a pivotal role in our daily lives, from our work life with emails and online systems, to our personal life with banking and shopping. This is only set to increase, so our children will be heavily relying on the Internet throughout their lives, from personal usage to academia and professional usage. Their proficiency with digital technology is somewhat imperative nowadays for them to function in society, to thrive and to succeed. Rather than forbidding its usage altogether, we suggest a handholding approach, whereby you introduce them slowly to the Internet in a controlled environment. As a parent, you can monitor their activity and oversee their transition into being a responsible Internet user – equipping them with an invaluable life skill while protecting them and empowering them to protect themselves.

13

Appendix

Glossary

References

Glossary

5:1 Rule: A guideline for the amount of time being spent online, based on extensive research. 5 hours of real world activity such as playing outdoors with friends, drawing, reading, doing homework etc., to 1 hour of 'screen time'

Active mediation: Discussing and encouraging open dialogue about a topic or medium

Blue light: Blue wavelengths which are omitted from screens when in use (e.g. Smartphones, televisions, laptops, tablets, iPods etc.). Blue light has been shown to disrupt sleep patterns significantly, particularly when exposed to blue light around bedtime

Chatbudi: A family member or friend who is over 18 and appointed by your child as their go-to person to talk to about their digital experiences. They share their positive and negative experiences with this individual, and agree to confide in them if they find themselves in a negative situation online

Cheats for games: Shortcuts, keyboard sequences, hints or downloads that help the player progress quicker than they would do normally, or to access characters, items or levels in the game that they would not otherwise

CoD: Call of Duty. It is a first-person shooter game franchise set in a warzone (usually either World War II, or a modern warzone), and available across a range of consoles and devices. The age rating is 16-18 depending on the version, and there are over 20 titles in the franchise at present

COPPA: The Child Online Privacy Protection Act is American legislation which applies to the online collection of personal information from children under 13 years of age; what a website operate must include in a privacy policy; when and how to seek verifiable parental consent, and includes marketing restrictions to under 13s.

Digital footprint: The trail or 'footprints' an Internet user leaves behind as they search the Internet. It can be passive, where information is gathered from our online behavior without us knowing (the sites we visit, products that interest us etc.) or active, where we voluntarily disclose information about ourselves (on social media, signing up to newsletters etc.)

Digital literacy: Possessing the knowledge, skills and ability to find, use, share and create content using digital technology and the Internet

Digital shadow: Another term for digital footprint, see above

f.lux: A computer program that adjusts the blue light being omitted by a screen in line with natural daylight. Designed to reduce the strain on the user's eyes and reduce the disruption to sleep patterns that is caused by blue light

Golden Rule: Real friends = virtual friends. In other words, your child should not be interacting with strangers online, and their online friends should be people that they know in the real world

Memory consolidation: The processes that stabilise a memory trace after it has been acquired. It is essentially the transfer of short-term memory into longer-term memory

Negative adjustment: When an individual reacts negatively to a change in environment or circumstances, employs negative coping strategies or reacts outside the accepted social norm

Restrictive mediation: Setting rules that restrict or prohibit the use of the medium

Screen time: Time spent on front of a screen or a device with a screen, such as a television, a laptop, a smartphone, a tablet, an iPod etc.

Self-isolation: Isolating oneself from social situations, from social environments and even from other people

Snapchat "discover": A feature on Snapchat which allows various publishers to show a daily edition of 5-10 curated stories, which refreshes every 24 hours. Publishers include Sky News and Sky Sports, MTV, Mail Online, BuzzFeed and Cosmopolitan

Snapchat "story": An individual Snap or a sequential string of 'snaps' put together to create a video that lasts for 24 hours (usually 'snaps' just play for

216   Zeeko Internet Safety Guide

the selected time when the recipient opens them and then disappear). Depending on privacy settings, a user's story can be viewed by all Snapchatters, just the user's friends or a selected group

Technostress: Anxiety or mental pressure stemming from overexposure or overreliance on technology

Tell No Blame: An approach to encourage a child to tell the truth, without fear of blame or serious punishment in order to learn from the issue

References

American Academy of Pediatrics. 'Media And Children'. N.p., Web. 20 Sept. 2015.

British Broadcast Corporation. 'BBC Three Survey - Porn: What's The Harm?'. N.p., Web. 20 Sept. 2015

Federal Trade Commission. Children's Online Privacy Protection Act of 1998

Katella-Cofrancesco, Kathy. (2012). 'Kids Need To Turn Off The Cell Phone Long Before Bed'. Yale School of Medicine

Livingstone, S. et al. (2013) 'In Their Own Words: What Bothers Children Online?'. EU Kids Online

Newzoo. (2014) 'Top 100 Countries Represent 99.8% of $81.5Bn Global Games Market'. N.p., Web. 20 Sept. 2015.

NSPCC. (2015) 'Online Porn: Evidence of Its Impact On Young People'. N.p., Web. 20 Sept. 2015.

Przybylski, A. K. (2014) 'Electronic Gaming and Psychosocial Adjustment'. PEDIATRICS Vol 134 No. 3

Rasch, Bjorn, and Jan Born. (2013) 'About Sleep's Role In Memory'. American Psychological Society

14

Index

Index

5 to 1 Rule, 116, 117
accounts, 146
Active mediation, 28, 51, 52, 85, 214
administrators, 67, 84
AirDrop, 140
American Physiological Society, 118
Android, 21, 70, 75, 79, 81, 118, 126, 132, 136, 151, 156, 157
   Parental Controls, 152
antisocial behaviour, 63, 64
app, 26, 32, 33, 37, 38, 47, 49, 50, 70, 92, 94, 106, 118, 125, 132, 145, 151, 154, 157, 180, 192
App Store, 132
Apple ID, 149
Apple Mac, 136, 176
   Apps, 176, 180
   Create a User, 176
   Logs, 186
   Other, 176, 185
   Parental Controls, 176
   People, 176, 183
   Set Parental Controls, 179
   Time Limits, 176, 184
   Web, 176, 181
AppLock, 132
AT&T, 124
Background App Refresh, 146
BBC, 194
block, 38, 54, 66, 67, 69, 70, 71, 74, 78, 80, 96, 124, 128, 173, 174, 181, 182
blue light, 34, 117, 118, 215

Bluetooth Sharing, 144
bystanders, 83
Calendars, 144
Call of Duty, 101, 103, 104, 106, 107, 214
   CoD, 101, 103, 106, 107, 108, 214
CarPlay, 140
Catfish, 94
chat apps, 25, 26, 27
Chatbudi, 54, 55, 65, 81, 85, 197, 210, 214
check-ins, 60
Childline, 194
Children's Online Privacy Protection Act, 33, 218
cognitive disconnection, 90
Common Sense Media, 105, 203, 204
Cyberbully, 19, 20, 27, 37, 39, 46, 54, 58, 59, 60, 62, 63, 82, 83, 84, 85, 86, 106, 204
   Accidental, 59
   Angry, 61
   Real, 63
cyberspace, 25, 27
digital citizen, 122
digital footprint, 19, 24, 25, 64, 215
Digital Safety Contract, 96
digital shadow, 24
digital technology, 25
Digiweb, 124
Discover, 50
Dock, 180

Eircom, 124
eMobile, 126
Excessive internet use, 20, 101, 102, 106, 107, 112, 113, 114, 115, 116, 132
f.lux, 118, 215
Facebook, 24, 35, 39, 40, 64, 67, 71, 124
FaceTime, 140
Family Sharing, 148, 150
FIFA, 26
Fritzbox 7360, 124
Game Center, 146, 180, 183
gamer, 49, 93
Gentile, Dr. Douglas, 101
Ghost Recon, 103
Gmail, 127, 129
Google, 127, 128, 129, 160
　Chrome, 128, 130
　Google Junior, 130
　Google Kids, 130
　Google Play, 156
Grand Theft Auto, 103, 104, 107
grooming, 204
Halo, 103
iBooks, 141
iCloud, 148, 149, 150
iKydz, 124
In-App Purchases, 141
Inappropriate content, 21, 27, 37, 40, 101, 103, 104, 106, 107, 128, 130, 132, 181, 182, 190, 191, 192, 193, 195, 196, 198
Insafe, 205, 206
Instagram, 20, 26, 32, 35, 37, 47, 49, 50, 64, 67, 70, 94

Internet, 4, 15, 16, 19, 21, 24, 25, 27, 28, 36, 41, 47, 52, 53, 58, 60, 64, 85, 86, 91, 107, 111, 112, 113, 116, 122, 123, 124, 131, 140, 181, 182, 183, 195, 196, 202, 207, 210, 211, 215
Internet Explorer, 130
Internet Matters, 204
iOS, 21, 70, 132, 136, 137, 148, 151
iPad, 19, 21, 25, 137, 148, 197
iPhone, 21, 72, 79, 80, 137, 148
iPod, 19, 21, 25, 117, 137, 214, 216
Irish Cellular Industry Association, 125
Irish Internet Safety Awareness Centre, 206
iTunes, 141, 148, 150
Jelly Bean, 157
junk mail, 181
K9 Web Protection, 131
Kid Mode, 132
KidRex, 130
Kids Place, 132
LinkedIn, 24
Location Services, 144
Location Settings, 144
Mandela, Nelson, 210
melatonin, 117, 118
Meteor, 126
Microphone, 145
Minecraft, 93, 101, 105, 106, 107
Mobicip, 131
Mobile Data Use, 146
Mobile Fence, 132
Mozilla Firefox, 130

Multiplayer Games, 146
Naomi, 131
Net Nanny, 131
Newzoo, 100, 218
NSPCC, 194
Oberlin College of Computer Science, 115
Ofcom, 204
online games, 25, 26, 55, 66, 93, 96, 174
online gaming, 20, 27, 49, 96, 101, 102
Parent's Crash Course, 136
PDST, Professional Development Service for Teachers, 206
PEGI, Pan European Game Information, 154
Play Store, 132, 151, 154, 160
podcasts, 141, 142
pornography, 125, 194, 195, 197, 198
posts, 60, 64
privacy settings, 54, 144, 217
Professional Development Service for Teachers, 206
profile, 24, 26, 33, 37, 38, 39, 40, 42, 54, 64, 67, 68, 69, 70, 71, 84, 86, 94, 96, 157, 159, 161, 172
Przybylski, Dr Andrew K., 102
Ranger Browser, 131
real friends = virtual friends, 51
Reminders, 144
Restrictive mediation, 52
RTA, Restricted to Adults, 182
Safari, 140, 183
Safer Internet Centre, 204

Safer Internet Day, 205, 207
SafeSearch, 128, 129
SafeSurf, 126, 182
Safety Net, 126
safety settings, 21, 33, 37, 39, 84, 121, 122, 123, 124, 126, 127, 128, 131, 136, 137, 140, 161, 176, 206, 211
screen time, 116, 117, 118, 214
screenshot, 39, 49
self-harm, 125
sexting, 204
Share My Location, 144
Simple Finder, 180
Simpsons Hit & Run, 104
Siri, 140, 142
Sky, 124, 216
Skype, 47
smartphone, 117, 216
Snapchat, 19, 26, 32, 35, 36, 38, 39, 47, 49, 50, 67, 68, 69, 124, 216
SnapCrack, 39
Snaps, 36, 39, 49, 50, 216
SnapSave, 39
social media, 24, 25, 26, 27, 32, 33, 34, 36, 40, 41, 42, 43, 47, 60, 61, 66, 84, 94, 96
social media profile, 24, 26
social networks, 32, 34, 204
Spyrix, 131
SSL, Secure Sockets Layer, 183
statuses, 60
Steam, 108
Stop Block Tell, 20, 42, 65, 83
Stranger Danger, 20, 89, 90, 91, 92, 93, 94, 95, 101

strangers online, 20, 90, 91, 93, 95, 216
tablet, 25, 117, 157, 216
tagging, 60
Talking Angela, 92
tech whiz, 47, 55
Technostress, 115, 217
Tell No Blame, 53, 217
T-Shirt Rule, 61
Viber, 32, 47, 49, 67, 79
virtual friend, 49, 54
Vodafone, 124, 126
Volume Limit, 146
Webwise, 206
WhatsApp, 36, 49, 67, 72
whitelist, 181
Wi-Fi, 19, 25, 26, 123, 125
Windows, 21, 70, 136, 161, 162, 165, 169, 172
    Accounts, 163

Add a child's account, 164
Apps & Games, 174
Block Inappropriate Website Function, 173
Family Safety website, 168
safety settings, 173
Screen Time, 175
Settings, 162
User Accounts and Family Safety, 161, 167
Windows Live Family Safety, 161
Xbox, 25
Yale Medical Group, 34
Young, Dr Kimberly, 113
YouTube, 27, 35, 47, 127
Zeeko
    Safe Communication App, 132
Zeeko.ie, 202